Casseroles

BOOKS

RDA ENTHUSIAST BRANDS, LLC
MILWAUKEE, WI

Casseroles

EDITORIAL
EDITOR-IN-CHIEF Catherine Cassidy
CREATIVE DIRECTOR Howard Greenberg
EDITORIAL OPERATIONS DIRECTOR Kerri Balliet

MANAGING EDITOR/PRINT & DIGITAL BOOKS Mark Hagen
ASSOCIATE CREATIVE DIRECTOR Edwin Robles Jr.

ASSOCIATE EDITOR Molly Jasinski
LAYOUT DESIGNER Courtney Lovetere
EDITORIAL PRODUCTION MANAGER Dena Ahlers
COPY CHIEF Deb Warlaumont Mulvey
COPY EDITOR Joanne Weintraub

FOOD EDITORS James Schend; Peggy Woodward, RD
RECIPE EDITORS Mary King; Jenni Sharp, RD; Irene Yeh
CONTENT OPERATIONS ASSISTANT Shannon Stroud
EDITORIAL SERVICES ADMINISTRATOR Marie Brannon

TEST KITCHEN & FOOD STYLING MANAGER
Sarah Thompson
TEST COOKS Nicholas Iverson (lead), Matthew Hass,
Lauren Knoelke
FOOD STYLISTS Kathryn Conrad (lead), Shannon Roum,
Leah Rekau
PREP COOKS Bethany Van Jacobson (lead), Megumi Garcia,
Melissa Hansen, Sara Wirtz

PHOTOGRAPHY DIRECTOR Stephanie Marchese
PHOTOGRAPHERS Dan Roberts, Jim Wieland
PHOTOGRAPHER/SET STYLIST Grace Natoli Sheldon
SET STYLISTS Stacey Genaw, Melissa Haberman, Dee Dee Jacq
PHOTO STUDIO ASSISTANT Ester Robards

EDITORIAL BUSINESS MANAGER Kristy Martin
EDITORIAL BUSINESS ASSOCIATE Samantha Lea Stoeger

EDITOR, *TASTE OF HOME* Jeanne Ambrose
ASSOCIATE CREATIVE DIRECTOR, *TASTE OF HOME*
Erin Burns
ART DIRECTOR, *TASTE OF HOME* Kristin Bowker

BUSINESS
VICE PRESIDENT, GROUP PUBLISHER Kirsten Marchioli
PUBLISHER, *TASTE OF HOME* Donna Lindskog
GENERAL MANAGER, TASTE OF HOME COOKING SCHOOL
Erin Puariea
EXECUTIVE PRODUCER, TASTE OF HOME ONLINE
COOKING SCHOOL Karen Berner

THE READER'S DIGEST ASSOCIATION, INC.
PRESIDENT AND CHIEF EXECUTIVE OFFICER Bonnie Kintzer
VICE PRESIDENT, CHIEF OPERATING OFFICER,
NORTH AMERICA Howard Halligan
CHIEF REVENUE OFFICER Richard Sutton
CHIEF MARKETING OFFICER Leslie Dukker Doty
VICE PRESIDENT, CONTENT MARKETING & OPERATIONS
Diane Dragan
SENIOR VICE PRESIDENT, GLOBAL HR & COMMUNICATIONS
Phyllis E. Gebhardt, SPHR
VICE PRESIDENT, BRAND MARKETING Beth Gorry
VICE PRESIDENT, CHIEF TECHNOLOGY OFFICER
Aneel Tejwaney
VICE PRESIDENT, CONSUMER MARKETING PLANNING
Jim Woods

COVER PHOTOGRAPHY
PHOTOGRAPHER Dan Roberts
FOOD STYLIST Dee Dee Jacq
SET STYLIST Kathryn Conrad

© 2015 RDA ENTHUSIAST BRANDS, LLC
1610 N. 2ND ST., SUITE 102, MILWAUKEE WI 53212-3906

INTERNATIONAL STANDARD BOOK NUMBER:
978-1-61765-459-6

LIBRARY OF CONGRESS CONTROL NUMBER: 2015937041

COMPONENT NUMBER: 116000216H00

PICTURED ON THE FRONT COVER:
Favorite Baked Spaghetti (p. 17)

PICTURED ON THE BACK COVER (FROM TOP):
Baked French Toast with Strawberries (p. 95); Greek Zucchini & Feta
Bake (p. 81); Simple Creamy Chicken Enchiladas (p. 41)

Dig Into Comfort!

When you're searching for a recipe that's hearty, simple and family-friendly, look no further than a tasty casserole. Bubbling hot bakes are sure to meet all your needs!

Inside *Taste of Home Casseroles,* you'll find **172 dishes** to satisfy your family at breakfast, lunch or dinner. Here's the best part: Home cooks just like you shared the recipes, which means these casseroles are inviting and easy to make! So let's get cooking!

Intrigued by the cheesy goodness on the cover? Find **Favorite Baked Spaghetti (p. 17)** in the first chapter. You also can't go wrong with **Buffalo Chicken Pasta Bake (p. 33), Sweet Potato Chili Bake (p. 74)** or **Twice-Baked Cheddar Potato Casserole (p. 107).**

Be on the lookout for recipes with FREEZE IT, FAST FIX and ⑤INGREDIENTS icons, too. If you're looking for a casserole you can have on the table in less than 30 minutes, you'll find a super-fast fix in tasty **Turkey & Spinach Stuffing Casserole (p. 39).** For a recipe to freeze now and heat up later, you'll love **Sausage Lasagna Rolls (p. 54).**

Need to get sleepyheads out of bed? There's nothing like the aroma of a home-cooked breakfast, and what's better than starting the day with a five-ingredient recipe such as **Picante Omelet Pie (p. 94)** or **Corny Beef Brunch (p. 89)**?

It's never been easier to find a new favorite—no matter what meal you're planning. With so many options to choose from, *Casseroles* will be your go-to cookbook for years to come!

87

33

85

31

52

39

Contents

LOOK FOR THESE HANDY ICONS:

FREEZE IT
With a little planning, you can make these casserole dishes ahead of time and simply store them in your freezer.

⑤ INGREDIENTS
With the exception of water, salt, pepper and oil, these dishes call for only a few items, many of which you likely have on hand.

FAST FIX
Eat great even on your busiest days. Discover easy recipes that are table-ready in 30 minutes or less!

LIKE US
facebook.com/tasteofhome

TWEET US
@tasteofhome

SHOP WITH US
shoptasteofhome.com

FOLLOW US
pinterest.com/taste_of_home

SHARE A RECIPE
tasteofhome.com/submit

DISCOVER MORE *TASTE OF HOME* CASSEROLE RECIPES ON FACEBOOK, PINTEREST *&* TWITTER

MARJORIE CAREY'S THREE-CHEESE JUMBO SHELLS *PAGE 22*

Beef & Ground Beef

NEED A DISH TO SATISFY YOUR ENTIRE CROWD?
LOOK NO FURTHER THAN THESE HEARTY CASSEROLE RECIPES.

VERLYN WILSON'S CHURCH SUPPER SPAGHETTI *PAGE 12*

JANINE TALLEY'S SHORT RIB COBBLER *PAGE 20*

STACY CIZEK'S CHEDDAR BEEF ENCHILADAS *PAGE 16*

Cavatini Pasta

This recipe has been in my family as long as I can remember, and it's still a favorite. I love to make it when we have company, because it's always a winner.

—RUSS PALMER SARANAC, MI

PREP: 30 MIN. + SIMMERING • **BAKE:** 35 MIN.
MAKES: 14 SERVINGS

- 2 pounds ground beef
- 2 medium onions, chopped
- 1 medium green pepper, chopped
- 6 garlic cloves, minced
- 4 cups water
- 1 can (12 ounces) tomato paste
- 1 can (4 ounces) mushroom stems and pieces, drained
- 1 package (3½ ounces) sliced pepperoni
- 2 envelopes spaghetti sauce mix
- 1 teaspoon Italian seasoning

PASTA
- 8 cups water
- 1 cup each uncooked elbow macaroni, bow tie pasta and medium pasta shells
- 2 cups (8 ounces) shredded part-skim mozzarella cheese

1. In a Dutch oven, cook the beef, onions and pepper over medium heat until meat is no longer pink; drain. Add garlic; cook 1 minute longer. Stir in water, tomato paste, mushrooms, pepperoni, sauce mix and Italian seasoning. Bring to a boil. Reduce heat; simmer, uncovered, for 1 hour.
2. Meanwhile, for pasta, bring water to a boil in a large saucepan. Add macaroni and pastas. Return to a boil, stirring occasionally. Cook, uncovered, for 10-12 minutes or until tender; drain. Stir into tomato sauce. Transfer to a greased 13x9-in. baking dish (dish will be full).
3. Bake at 350° for 30 minutes. Sprinkle with cheese. Bake 5-10 minutes longer or until cheese is melted.

OLE POLENTA CASSEROLE

Ole Polenta Casserole

This casserole has been popular in our home for years. I like to put a dollop of sour cream on each serving.

—ANGELA BIGGIN LYONS, IL

PREP: 1 HOUR + CHILLING
BAKE: 40 MIN. + STANDING
MAKES: 6 SERVINGS

- 1 cup yellow cornmeal
- 1 teaspoon salt
- 4 cups water, divided
- 1 pound ground beef
- 1 cup chopped onion
- ½ cup chopped green pepper
- 2 garlic cloves, minced
- 1 can (14½ ounces) diced tomatoes, undrained
- 1 can (8 ounces) tomato sauce
- ½ pound sliced fresh mushrooms
- 1 teaspoon each dried basil, oregano and dill weed
  Dash hot pepper sauce
- 1½ cups (6 ounces) shredded part-skim mozzarella cheese
- ¼ cup grated Parmesan cheese

1. For polenta, in a small bowl, whisk the cornmeal, salt and 1 cup water until smooth. In a large saucepan, bring remaining water to a boil. Add cornmeal mixture, stirring constantly. Bring to a boil; cook and stir for 3 minutes or until thickened.
2. Reduce heat to low; cover and cook for 15 minutes. Divide mixture between two greased 8-in.-square baking dishes. Cover and refrigerate until firm, about 1½ hours.
3. In a large skillet, cook the beef, onion, green pepper and garlic over medium heat until meat is no longer pink; drain. Stir in the tomatoes, tomato sauce, mushrooms, herbs and hot pepper sauce; bring to a boil. Reduce heat; simmer, uncovered, for 20 minutes or until thickened.
4. Loosen one polenta from sides and bottom of dish; invert onto a waxed paper-lined baking sheet and set aside. Spoon half of the meat mixture over the remaining polenta. Sprinkle with half the mozzarella and half the Parmesan cheese. Top with reserved polenta and remaining meat mixture.
5. Cover and bake at 350° for 40 minutes or until heated through. Uncover; sprinkle with remaining cheese. Bake 5 minutes longer or until cheese is melted. Let stand for 10 minutes before cutting.

Spinach Beef Macaroni Bake

I serve this dish at big family gatherings and church suppers. If you cut the recipe in half, it's good for smaller family dinners. My grandson-in-law and great-grandson often ask me to whip it up when they stop by to visit.

—**LOIS LAUPPE** LAHOMA, OK

PREP: 55 MIN. • **BAKE:** 25 MIN.
MAKES: 2 CASSEROLES
(12 SERVINGS EACH)

- 5¼ cups uncooked elbow macaroni
- 2½ pounds ground beef
- 2 large onions, chopped
- 3 large carrots, shredded
- 3 celery ribs, chopped
- 2 cans (28 ounces each) Italian diced tomatoes, undrained
- 4 teaspoons salt
- 1 teaspoon garlic powder
- 1 teaspoon pepper
- ½ teaspoon dried oregano
- 2 packages (10 ounces each) frozen chopped spinach, thawed and squeezed dry
- 1 cup grated Parmesan cheese

1. Cook macaroni according to package directions. Meanwhile, in a large Dutch oven, cook the beef, onions, carrots and celery over medium heat until meat is no longer pink; drain. Add the tomatoes, salt, garlic powder, pepper and oregano. Bring to a boil. Reduce heat; cover and simmer for 30 minutes or until vegetables are tender.

2. Drain macaroni; add macaroni and spinach to beef mixture. Pour into two greased 3-qt. baking dishes. Sprinkle with cheese. Bake, uncovered, at 350° for 25-30 minutes or until heated through.

FREEZE IT

Chipotle Mac & Cheese

Beefy and bubbly, this Southwestern pasta bake heats dinner up a notch with a chipotle-pepper kick.

—**CYNDY GERKEN** NAPLES, FL

PREP: 35 MIN. • **BAKE:** 30 MIN.
MAKES: 2 CASSEROLES (4 SERVINGS EACH)

- 1 package (16 ounces) spiral pasta
- 2 pounds ground beef
- 2 large onions, chopped
- 2 large green peppers, chopped
- 3 garlic cloves, minced
- 1 can (28 ounces) crushed tomatoes
- 1 can (10¾ ounces) condensed cheddar cheese soup, undiluted
- ½ cup 2% milk
- 1 chipotle pepper in adobo sauce, chopped
- 2 tablespoons chili powder
- 1 tablespoon ground cumin
- 1 teaspoon cayenne pepper
- 1 teaspoon dried oregano
- ½ teaspoon salt
- ¼ teaspoon pepper
- 2 cups (8 ounces) shredded Monterey Jack cheese
- 2 tablespoons minced fresh cilantro, optional

1. Cook pasta according to package directions to al dente. Meanwhile, in a Dutch oven, cook beef, onions, green peppers and garlic over medium heat until meat is no longer pink. Drain.

2. Stir in the tomatoes, soup, milk, chipotle pepper and seasonings. Bring to a boil. Reduce heat; cover and simmer for 15 minutes or until thickened.

3. Drain pasta; stir into meat mixture. Divide between two greased 8-in-square baking dishes; sprinkle with cheese and, if desired, cilantro.

4. Cover and freeze one casserole for up to 3 months. Cover and bake the remaining casserole at 350° for 20 minutes. Uncover; bake 8-10 minutes longer or until bubbly and cheese is melted.

TO USE FROZEN CASSEROLE *Thaw in the refrigerator overnight. Remove from the refrigerator 30 minutes before baking. Cover and bake at 350° for 60 minutes. Uncover; bake 8-10 minutes longer or until bubbly and cheese is melted.*

SPINACH BEEF MACARONI BAKE

Broccoli Biscuit Squares

With a biscuitlike crust, these pretty squares disappear quickly at our house. We enjoy them for dinner or breakfast.

—VI JANUS PELICAN LAKE, WI

PREP: 25 MIN. • **BAKE:** 25 MIN.
MAKES: 6 SERVINGS

- 1 **pound ground beef**
- 1 **can (4 ounces) mushroom stems and pieces, drained**
- 1 **small onion, chopped**
- 2 **cups biscuit/baking mix**
- 2 **cups (8 ounces) shredded cheddar cheese, divided**
- ¼ **cup grated Parmesan cheese**
- ½ **cup water**
- 3 **cups frozen chopped broccoli, thawed and drained**
- 4 **eggs**
- ½ **cup milk**
- 1 **teaspoon salt**
  Dash pepper

1. In a large skillet, cook the beef, mushrooms and onion over medium heat until meat is no longer pink; drain. In a large bowl, combine the biscuit mix, ½ cup cheddar cheese, Parmesan cheese and water until a soft dough forms.

2. Press dough onto the bottom and ½ in. up the sides of a greased 13x9-in. baking dish. Stir remaining cheddar cheese into the beef mixture; spread over dough. Sprinkle with broccoli.

3. In a large bowl, beat eggs, milk, salt and pepper. Pour over meat mixture. Bake, uncovered, at 400° for 25 minutes or until a knife inserted near center comes out clean.

DID YOU KNOW?

Not sure what a "dash" is? When a recipe calls for a dash of an ingredient, it's a very small amount of seasoning added with a quick downward stroke of the hand.

BROCCOLI BISCUIT SQUARES

Tater Tot Casseroles

Ground beef, cheese and, of course, Tater Tots make these homey casseroles real crowd-pleasers. Cayenne pepper and hot Italian sausage give them an extra punch.
—**RYAN JONES** CHILLICOTHE, IL

PREP: 25 MIN. • **BAKE:** 45 MIN.
MAKES: 2 CASSEROLES (6 SERVINGS EACH)

- ¾ **pound bulk hot Italian sausage**
- ¾ **pound lean ground beef (90% lean)**
- 1 **small onion, chopped**
- 2 **cans (10¾ ounces each) condensed cream of celery soup, undiluted**
- 2 **cups frozen cut green beans, thawed**
- 1 **can (15¼ ounces) whole kernel corn, drained**
- 2 **cups (8 ounces) shredded Colby-Monterey Jack cheese, divided**
- ½ **cup 2% milk**
- 1 **teaspoon garlic powder**
- ¼ **teaspoon seasoned salt**
- ¼ to ½ **teaspoon cayenne pepper**
- 1 **package (32 ounces) frozen Tater Tots**

1. In a Dutch oven, cook the sausage, beef and onion over medium heat until meat is no longer pink; drain. Add the soup, beans, corn, 1 cup cheese, milk, garlic powder, seasoned salt and cayenne. Transfer to two greased 11x7-in. baking dishes. Top with Tater Tots; sprinkle with remaining cheese.

2. Cover and freeze one casserole for up to 3 months. Cover and bake the remaining casserole at 350° for 40 minutes. Uncover and bake 5-10 minutes longer or until bubbly.

TO USE FROZEN CASSEROLE *Thaw in the refrigerator overnight. Remove from the refrigerator 30 minutes before baking. Cover and bake at 350° for 50 minutes. Uncover and bake 5-10 minutes longer or until bubbly.*

Mexi-Mac Casserole

Here's one of my favorite all-in-one meals. Green chilies add a little bite, but swap in a spicier can of tomatoes if you want to turn up the heat.
—**JAN CONKLIN** STEVENSVILLE, MT

PREP: 25 MIN. • **BAKE:** 30 MIN.
MAKES: 8 SERVINGS

- 1 **package (7¼ ounces) macaroni and cheese dinner mix**
- 1½ **pounds lean ground beef (90% lean)**
- 1 **medium onion, finely chopped**
- 2 **garlic cloves, minced**
- 1 **can (14½ ounces) diced tomatoes with mild green chilies**
- 1 **can (4 ounces) chopped green chilies**
- 1 **envelope reduced-sodium taco seasoning**
- 2½ **cups (10 ounces) shredded Mexican cheese blend, divided**
- 1 **can (16 ounces) kidney beans, rinsed and drained**
- 1 **can (15¼ ounces) whole kernel corn, drained**
- 1 **can (7¾ ounces) Mexican-style hot tomato sauce**
- ½ **cup crushed tortilla chips**

1. Prepare the macaroni and cheese mix according to package directions. Meanwhile, cook the beef, onion and garlic in a Dutch oven over medium heat until meat is no longer pink; drain.

2. Add the diced tomatoes, green chilies and taco seasoning. Stir in 2 cups cheese, beans, corn, tomato sauce and prepared macaroni and cheese dinner.

3. Transfer to a greased 13x9-in. baking dish; sprinkle with chips and remaining cheese.

4. Bake, uncovered, at 350° for 30-35 minutes or until bubbly.

FREEZE OPTION *Cool unbaked casserole; cover and freeze. To use, partially thaw in refrigerator overnight. Remove from refrigerator 30 minutes before baking. Preheat oven to 350°. Bake casserole as directed, increasing time as necessary to heat through and for a thermometer inserted in center to read 165°.*

MEXI-MAC CASSEROLE

FAST FIX

Stovetop Hamburger Casserole

This recipe is about enjoying comfort food at its best. It's not only loaded with ground beef, pasta, veggies and cheddar cheese, it also goes together in a jiffy.

—EDITH LANDINGER LONGVIEW, TX

START TO FINISH: 25 MIN.
MAKES: 6 SERVINGS

- 1 package (7 ounces) small pasta shells
- 1½ pounds ground beef
- 1 large onion, chopped
- 3 medium carrots, chopped
- 1 celery rib, chopped
- 3 garlic cloves, minced
- 3 cups cubed cooked red potatoes
- 1 can (15¼ ounces) whole kernel corn, drained
- 2 cans (8 ounces each) tomato sauce
- 1½ teaspoons salt
- ½ teaspoon pepper
- 1 cup (4 ounces) shredded cheddar cheese

1. Cook pasta according to package directions. Meanwhile, in a large skillet, cook beef and onion over medium heat until meat is no longer pink; drain. Add carrots and celery; cook and stir for 5 minutes or until vegetables are crisp-tender. Add garlic; cook 1 minute longer.
2. Stir in the potatoes, corn, tomato sauce, salt and pepper; heat through. Drain pasta and add to skillet; toss to coat. Sprinkle with cheese. Cover and cook until cheese is melted.

Church Supper Spaghetti

Because this sensational recipe feeds so many, I often take it to church dinners. The colorful dish also comes in handy when we have lots of helpers on our farm to feed.

—VERLYN WILSON WILKINSON, IN

PREP: 50 MIN. • **BAKE:** 20 MIN.
MAKES: 12 SERVINGS

- 1 pound ground beef
- 1 large onion, chopped
- 1 medium green pepper, chopped
- 1 can (14½ ounces) diced tomatoes, undrained
- 1 cup water
- 2 tablespoons chili powder
- 1 package (10 ounces) frozen corn, thawed
- 1 package (10 ounces) frozen peas, thawed
- 1 can (4 ounces) mushroom stems and pieces, drained
   Salt and pepper to taste
- 1 package (12 ounces) spaghetti, cooked and drained
- 2 cups (8 ounces) shredded cheddar cheese, divided

1. In a large skillet, cook beef, onion and green pepper over medium heat until meat is no longer pink. Add tomatoes, water and chili powder. Cover and simmer for 30 minutes. Add the corn, peas, mushrooms, salt and pepper. Stir in spaghetti.
2. Layer half of the mixture in a greased 4-qt. baking dish. Sprinkle with 1 cup cheese; repeat layers.
3. Bake, uncovered, at 350° for 20 minutes or until heated through.

STOVETOP HAMBURGER CASSEROLE

Burrito Lasagna

A friend showed me how to make stacked enchiladas years ago, so I gave her idea a twist with this hearty casserole, which is perfect for dinnertime.
—DEANA BRIGGS MAUD, TX

PREP: 35 MIN. • **BAKE:** 30 MIN. + STANDING
MAKES: 12 SERVINGS

- 2 **pounds ground beef**
- 2 **cans (10 ounces each) enchilada sauce**
- 1 **envelope taco seasoning**
- 1 **tablespoon ground cumin**
- 1 **package (8.8 ounces) ready-to-serve Spanish rice**
- 12 **flour tortillas (8 inches), warmed**
- 1 **can (15 ounces) refried beans**
- 4 **cups (16 ounces) shredded Mexican cheese blend**
  Optional toppings: salsa, sliced avocado, shredded lettuce, taco sauce and/or sour cream

1. Preheat oven to 350°. In a large skillet, cook beef over medium heat until no longer pink; drain. Stir in enchilada sauce, taco seasoning and cumin; heat through.

2. Heat rice according to package directions. Spread each tortilla with about 2 tablespoonfuls beans. Spread 1 cup meat mixture into a greased 13x9-in. baking dish. Layer with 4 tortillas and a third of the rice, a third of remaining meat mixture and a third of the cheese. Repeat layers. Top with the remaining tortillas, rice and meat mixture (dish will be full).

3. Cover and bake 20 minutes. Sprinkle with remaining cheese. Uncover; bake 10-15 minutes longer or until cheese is melted. Let stand 10 minutes before serving. Serve with toppings of your choice.

CABBAGE ROLL CASSEROLE

Cabbage Roll Casserole

I layer cabbage and a ground beef filling lasagna-style in this casserole that cabbage-roll lovers will savor.
—DOREEN MARTIN KITIMAT, BC

PREP: 20 MIN. • **BAKE:** 55 MIN.
MAKES: 12 SERVINGS

- 2 **pounds ground beef**
- 1 **large onion, chopped**
- 3 **garlic cloves, minced**
- 2 **cans (15 ounces each) tomato sauce, divided**
- 1 **teaspoon dried thyme**
- ½ **teaspoon dill weed**
- ½ **teaspoon rubbed sage**
- ¼ **teaspoon salt**
- ¼ **teaspoon pepper**
- ¼ **teaspoon cayenne pepper**
- 2 **cups cooked rice**
- 4 **bacon strips, cooked and crumbled**
- 1 **medium head cabbage (2 pounds), shredded**
- 1 **cup (4 ounces) shredded part-skim mozzarella cheese**

1. Preheat oven to 375°. In a large skillet, cook beef and onion over medium heat until meat is no longer pink. Add garlic; cook 1 minute longer. Drain. Stir in one can of tomato sauce and seasonings. Bring to a boil. Reduce heat; cover and simmer 5 minutes. Stir in the rice and bacon; heat through. Remove from heat.

2. Layer a third of the cabbage in a greased 13x9-in. baking dish. Top with half of the meat mixture. Repeat layers; top with the remaining cabbage. Pour remaining tomato sauce over top.

3. Cover and bake 45 minutes. Uncover; sprinkle with cheese. Bake 10 minutes longer or until cheese is melted. Let stand 5 minutes before serving.

Taco Casserole

My family always devours this casserole, which tastes like a taco salad.

—RHONDA MCKEE GREENSBURG, KS

PREP: 25 MIN. • **BAKE:** 15 MIN.
MAKES: 4 SERVINGS

- 1 pound ground beef
- ¼ cup chopped onion
- ¼ cup chopped green pepper
- 1 envelope taco seasoning
- ½ cup water
- 1 cup crushed tortilla chips
- 1 can (16 ounces) refried beans
- 1 cup (4 ounces) shredded cheddar cheese
    Toppings: chopped lettuce and tomatoes, sliced ripe olives, sour cream and picante sauce

1. In a large skillet, cook beef, onion and green pepper over medium heat until meat is no longer pink; drain. Stir in the taco seasoning and water. Cook and stir until thickened, about 3 minutes; set aside.

2. Place the chips in a greased 8-in.-square baking dish. In a small bowl, stir refried beans; spread over chips. Top with the beef mixture and cheese.

3. Bake, uncovered, at 375° for 15-20 minutes or until heated through. Top with lettuce, tomatoes and olives. Serve with sour cream and picante sauce.

MIDWEST MEATBALL CASSEROLE

Midwest Meatball Casserole

I've relied on this recipe many times as a soothing finish to a hectic day. Since I usually have all the ingredients on hand, there's no last-minute rush to the store to worry about, either.

—JUDY LARSON GREENDALE, WI

PREP: 15 MIN. • **BAKE:** 30 MIN.
MAKES: 6 SERVINGS

- 2 cans (8 ounces each) tomato sauce, divided
- 1 egg
- ¼ cup dry bread crumbs
- ¼ cup chopped onion
- 1 teaspoon salt
- 1 pound lean ground beef (90% lean)
- 1 package (10 ounces) frozen mixed vegetables
- ½ teaspoon dried thyme
- ⅛ teaspoon pepper
- 1 package (16 ounces) frozen shredded hash brown potatoes, thawed
- 1 tablespoon butter, melted
- 3 slices process American cheese slices, cut into ½-inch strips

1. In a large bowl, combine 2 tablespoons tomato sauce, egg, bread crumbs, onion and salt. Crumble beef over mixture and mix well. Shape into 1-in. balls.

2. Place meatballs on a greased rack in a shallow baking pan and bake at 375° for 15-20 minutes or until meatballs are no longer pink; drain.

3. Meanwhile, in a large skillet, combine remaining tomato sauce with vegetables and seasonings. Cover and simmer 10-15 minutes or until heated through; stir in meatballs and set aside.

4. Place potatoes in a greased 11x7-in. baking dish. Brush with butter and bake at 375° for 15-20 minutes or until lightly browned. Remove from the oven; top with meatball mixture. Arrange cheese strips in a lattice pattern on top. Bake, uncovered, for 20-25 minutes longer or until heated through and cheese is melted.

Swiss Steak with Dumplings

My mother was a great cook, and I learned so much from her. Ten years ago, I entered this hearty recipe in a contest and won. It's great all year and one of our workers' favorites when I take it to the field during harvest.

—PAT HABIGER SPEARVILLE, KS

PREP: 25 MIN. • **BAKE:** 70 MIN.
MAKES: 6-8 SERVINGS

- 2 pounds beef top round steak
- ⅓ cup all-purpose flour
- 2 tablespoons canola oil
- 2 cans (10¾ ounces each) condensed cream of chicken soup, undiluted
- 1⅓ cups water
- ½ teaspoon salt
- ⅛ teaspoon pepper

DUMPLINGS
- ½ cup dry bread crumbs
- 5 tablespoons butter, melted, divided
- 1⅓ cups all-purpose flour
- 2 teaspoons baking powder
- ½ teaspoon salt
- ¼ teaspoon poultry seasoning
- ⅔ cup milk

1. Cut steaks into six or eight pieces. Place flour in a large resealable bag. Add beef, a few pieces at a time, and shake to coat. In a large skillet, brown meat in oil on both sides. Transfer to a greased 2½-qt. baking dish.
2. In the same skillet, combine the soup, water, salt and pepper; bring to a boil, stirring occasionally. Pour over steak. Cover and bake at 350° for 50-60 minutes or until meat is tender.
3. For dumplings, combine bread crumbs and 2 tablespoons butter in a small bowl; set aside. In another bowl, combine the flour, baking powder, salt and poultry seasoning. Stir in milk and remaining butter just until moistened.
4. Drop by rounded tablespoonfuls into the crumb mixture; roll until coated. Place dumplings over steak. Bake, uncovered, at 425° for 20-30 minutes or until dumplings are lightly browned and a toothpick inserted near the center comes out clean.

SWEET-AND-SOUR SUPPER

Sweet-and-Sour Supper

My mother shared this recipe, which I've been making for my own family for years. The homemade sweet-and-sour sauce is the key to its success.

—DOROTHY REIMER DEWBERRY, AB

PREP: 20 MIN. • **BAKE:** 30 MIN.
MAKES: 4-6 SERVINGS

- 1 pound ground beef
- 1½ teaspoons chili powder
- 1½ teaspoons dried oregano
- 1½ teaspoons salt
  Pepper to taste
- 3 cups cooked long grain rice
- 1 can (7 ounces) mushroom stems and pieces, drained
- 1 medium green pepper, sliced

SAUCE
- 1 cup plus 2 tablespoons sugar
- ⅓ cup cornstarch
- 2½ cups cold water
- ⅓ cup white vinegar
- ⅓ cup ketchup
- 1½ teaspoons salt
  Pepper to taste

1. In a large skillet, cook beef over medium heat until meat is no longer pink; drain. Stir in the chili powder, oregano, salt and pepper.
2. In a greased 3-qt. baking dish, layer the rice, beef mixture, mushrooms and green pepper; set aside. In a large saucepan, combine sugar and cornstarch; stir in the remaining sauce ingredients until smooth. Bring to a boil; cook and stir for 2 minutes or until thickened.
3. Pour over layered ingredients. Bake, uncovered, at 350° for 30 minutes or until heated through.

LAYERED POTATO BEEF CASSEROLE

FREEZE IT

Cheddar Beef Enchiladas

I came up with these enchiladas to satisfy several picky eaters in our house. They were an instant hit. I especially like that we can enjoy this meal twice by freezing half for another busy day.
—**STACY CIZEK** CONRAD, IA

PREP: 30 MIN. • **BAKE:** 20 MIN.
MAKES: 2 CASSEROLES
(5-6 ENCHILADAS EACH)

- 1 **pound ground beef**
- 1 **envelope taco seasoning**
- 1 **cup water**
- 2 **cups cooked rice**
- 1 **can (16 ounces) refried beans**
- 2 **cups (8 ounces) shredded cheddar cheese, divided**
- 10 **to 12 flour tortillas (8 inches), warmed**
- 1 **jar (16 ounces) salsa**
- 1 **can (10¾ ounces) condensed cream of chicken soup, undiluted**

1. In a large skillet, cook beef over medium heat until no longer pink; drain. Stir in taco seasoning and water. Bring to a boil. Reduce heat; simmer, uncovered, for 5 minutes. Stir in rice. Cook and stir until liquid is evaporated.
2. Spread about 2 tablespoons of refried beans, ¼ cup beef mixture and 1 tablespoon cheese down the center of each tortilla; roll up. Place seam side down in two greased 13x9-in. baking dishes.
3. Combine salsa and soup; pour down the center of enchiladas. Sprinkle with remaining cheese.
4. Bake one casserole, uncovered, at 350° for 20-25 minutes or until heated through and cheese is melted. Cover and freeze remaining casserole for up to 3 months.
TO USE FROZEN CASSEROLE *Thaw in the refrigerator overnight. Cover and bake at 350° for 30 minutes. Uncover; bake 5-10 minutes longer or until heated through and cheese is melted.*

Layered Potato Beef Casserole

Beef and potatoes in a casserole? Talk about delicious! After a little bit of prep time, you'll have 50 minutes to relax before dinner.
—**MARGIE WILLIAMS** MOUNT JULIET, TN

PREP: 25 MIN. • **BAKE:** 50 MIN.
MAKES: 6 SERVINGS

- 3 **tablespoons butter, divided**
- 2 **tablespoons all-purpose flour**
- ¾ **teaspoon dried rosemary, crushed**
- ¼ **teaspoon pepper**
- ⅛ **teaspoon salt**
- 2 **cups 2% milk**
- 2 **cups (8 ounces) shredded sharp cheddar cheese**
- 4 **cups leftover beef stew**
- 4 **medium Yukon potatoes, thinly sliced**
- ⅓ **cup crushed butter-flavored crackers (about 8 crackers)**
- 1 **tablespoon dried parsley flakes**
- ¼ **teaspoon garlic powder**

1. Melt 2 tablespoons butter in a large saucepan. Stir in the flour, rosemary, pepper and salt until blended; gradually add milk. Bring to a boil; cook and stir for 2 minutes or until thickened. Remove from the heat; stir in cheese until melted.
2. Spoon 2 cups stew into a greased 2½-qt. baking dish. Layer with half of the potatoes and sauce mixture. Layer with remaining stew, potatoes and sauce.
3. Cover and bake at 400° for 45-50 minutes or until potatoes are tender. In a microwave, melt the remaining butter. Stir in the crackers, parsley and garlic powder. Sprinkle over casserole. Bake, uncovered, 5-10 minutes longer or until bubbly and topping is golden brown. Let stand for 10 minutes before serving.

Favorite Baked Spaghetti

Layering the spaghetti and sauce ensures that the pasta won't dry out if you're taking this to a potluck. This dish is popular with my grandchildren—they love the cheesiness.

—**LOUISE MILLER** WESTMINSTER, MD

PREP: 25 MIN. • **BAKE:** 1 HOUR
MAKES: 10 SERVINGS

- 1 **package (16 ounces) spaghetti**
- 1 **pound ground beef**
- 1 **medium onion, chopped**
- 1 **jar (24 ounces) meatless spaghetti sauce**
- ½ **teaspoon seasoned salt**
- 2 **eggs**
- ⅓ **cup grated Parmesan cheese**
- 5 **tablespoons butter, melted**
- 2 **cups (16 ounces) 4% cottage cheese**
- 4 **cups (16 ounces) part-skim shredded mozzarella cheese**

1. Cook spaghetti according to package directions. Meanwhile, in a large skillet, cook beef and onion over medium heat until meat is no longer pink; drain. Stir in spaghetti sauce and seasoned salt; set aside.

2. In a large bowl, whisk the eggs, Parmesan cheese and butter. Drain spaghetti; add to the egg mixture and toss to coat.

3. Place half of spaghetti mixture in a greased 3-qt. baking dish. Top with half of the cottage cheese, meat sauce and mozzarella cheese. Repeat layers.

4. Cover and bake at 350° for 40 minutes. Uncover; bake 20-25 minutes longer or until the cheese is melted.

CHEESEBURGER AND
FRIES CASSEROLE

ALFREDO TOPPING

- ¼ cup butter, cubed
- 2 tablespoons all-purpose flour
- 2 cups half-and-half cream
- 1 cup grated Parmesan cheese, divided
- 1 teaspoon minced fresh thyme or ¼ teaspoon dried thyme
- 1 teaspoon minced fresh oregano or ¼ teaspoon dried oregano

1. In a large bowl, combine egg, bread crumbs, water, cheese and seasonings. Crumble beef over mixture and mix well. Shape into 1½-in. balls. In a Dutch oven, brown meatballs in oil in batches; remove and keep warm.

2. Drain, reserving 1 tablespoon drippings. In drippings, saute the onion until tender. Add garlic; cook 1 minute longer. Add wine; cook and stir 3 minutes.

3. Return the meatballs to pan; stir in tomatoes and parsley. Bring to a boil. Reduce heat; cover and simmer 25-30 minutes or until meat is no longer pink.

4. Meanwhile, preheat oven to 400°. Cook rigatoni according to package directions.

5. In a small saucepan, melt butter. Stir in flour until smooth; gradually add cream. Bring to a boil; cook and stir 1-2 minutes or until thickened. Remove from heat. Stir in ¾ cup Parmesan cheese.

6. Drain rigatoni; place in a large bowl. Add meatballs and sauce; stir to coat. Transfer to a greased 13x9-in. baking dish.

7. Top with Alfredo sauce; sprinkle with thyme, oregano and remaining Parmesan cheese. Bake, uncovered, 20-25 minutes or until bubbly.

---

(5) INGREDIENTS

Cheeseburger and Fries Casserole

My kids love this casserole because it combines two of their favorite fast foods. I like the fact that I can whip it up with just four ingredients.

—KAREN OWEN RISING SUN, IN

PREP: 10 MIN. • **BAKE:** 50 MIN.
MAKES: 6-8 SERVINGS

- 2 pounds lean ground beef (90% lean)
- 1 can (10¾ ounces) condensed golden mushroom soup, undiluted
- 1 can (10¾ ounces) condensed cheddar cheese soup, undiluted
- 1 package (20 ounces) frozen crinkle-cut French fries

1. Preheat oven to 350°. In a large skillet, cook beef over medium heat until no longer pink; drain. Stir in soups. Pour into a greased 13x9-in. baking dish.

2. Arrange French fries on top. Bake, uncovered, 50-55 minutes or until the fries are golden brown.

Meatball Rigatoni Alfredo

My family can't get enough of meatballs with rigatoni or spaghetti. The baked cheese sauce takes it over the top!

—JENNIFER ROSS CLINTON, OH

PREP: 1¼ HOURS • **BAKE:** 20 MIN.
MAKES: 6 SERVINGS

- 1 egg, lightly beaten
- ¾ cup seasoned bread crumbs
- ⅓ cup water
- ¼ cup grated Parmesan cheese
- 4½ teaspoons each minced fresh thyme, oregano and basil or 1½ teaspoons each dried thyme, oregano and basil
- 1½ teaspoons pepper
- ½ teaspoon salt
- 1½ pounds ground beef
- 1 tablespoon canola oil
- 1 small onion, chopped
- 3 garlic cloves, minced
- ⅓ cup dry red wine or beef broth
- 1 can (28 ounces) crushed tomatoes
- 1 tablespoon minced fresh parsley
- 12 ounces uncooked rigatoni or large tube pasta

TOP TIP

Ground beef is often labeled with the cut of meat that it is ground from, like ground chuck or ground round. There may also be information on the fat content or the percentage of lean meat to fat, such as 85% or 90% lean. The higher the percentage, the leaner the meat.

Firecracker Casserole

Growing up, I couldn't get enough of this Southwestern casserole my mother frequently put on the dinner table. Now I fix it for my husband and me. The flavor reminds us of enchiladas. Have a fiesta for dinner tonight!

—TERESSA EASTMAN EL DORADO, KS

PREP: 15 MIN. • **BAKE:** 25 MIN.
MAKES: 8 SERVINGS

- 2 pounds ground beef
- 1 medium onion, chopped
- 1 can (15 ounces) black beans, rinsed and drained
- 1 to 2 tablespoons chili powder
- 2 to 3 teaspoons ground cumin
- ½ teaspoon salt
- 4 flour tortillas (6 inches)
- 1 can (10¾ ounces) condensed cream of mushroom soup, undiluted
- 1 can (10 ounces) diced tomatoes and green chilies, undrained
- 1 cup (4 ounces) shredded cheddar cheese

1. In a large skillet, cook beef and onion until the meat is no longer pink; drain. Add the beans, chili powder, cumin and salt.

2. Transfer to a greased 13x9-in. baking dish. Arrange tortillas over the top. Combine the soup and tomatoes; pour over tortillas. Sprinkle with cheese.

3. Bake, uncovered, at 350° for 25-30 minutes or until heated through.

Beef Stew with Sesame Seed Biscuits

Comfort food should be warm and hearty, and that's exactly what this dinner is about. The recipe has it all: homemade biscuits, tender meat and lots of veggies.

—LINDA BACCI LIVONIA, NY

PREP: 20 MIN. + SIMMERING • **BAKE:** 30 MIN.
MAKES: 5 SERVINGS

- 1 pound beef stew meat, cut into 1-inch cubes
- 2 tablespoons olive oil
- 1½ cups chopped onions
- 1 cup chopped celery
- 1 garlic clove, minced
- 1 tablespoon all-purpose flour
- 1½ cups water
- 1 cup diced tomatoes
- ½ cup Burgundy wine or beef broth
- ⅓ cup tomato paste
- 1 tablespoon sugar
- ¾ teaspoon salt
- ½ teaspoon Worcestershire sauce
- ¼ teaspoon pepper
- 2 cups cubed peeled potatoes
- 2 cups sliced fresh carrots
- 1 can (4 ounces) mushroom stems and pieces, drained
- ¼ cup sour cream

SESAME SEED BISCUITS
- 1¼ cups all-purpose flour
- 2 teaspoons baking powder
- ½ teaspoon salt
- ¼ cup shortening
- ¾ cup sour cream
- 2 tablespoons 2% milk
- 1 tablespoon sesame seeds

1. In a Dutch oven, brown the beef in oil in batches. Remove and keep warm. In the same pan, saute onions and celery until tender. Add garlic; cook 1 minute longer.

2. Stir in flour until blended. Gradually add water; stir in tomatoes, wine, tomato paste, sugar, salt, Worcestershire sauce, pepper and beef. Bring to a boil. Reduce heat; cover and simmer 1¼ hours.

3. Add potatoes and carrots; cook 30-45 minutes longer or until beef and vegetables are tender. Stir in mushrooms and sour cream. Transfer to a greased 13x9-in. baking dish.

4. Preheat oven to 400°. For biscuits, in a large bowl, combine flour, baking powder and salt. Cut in shortening until mixture resembles coarse crumbs. Stir in sour cream just until moistened.

5. Turn onto a lightly floured surface; knead 8-10 times. Roll out to ½-in. thickness; cut with a floured 2-in. biscuit cutter. Brush with milk; sprinkle with sesame seeds. Arrange over stew.

6. Bake 30-35 minutes or until biscuits are golden brown.

FIRECRACKER CASEROLE

REUBEN BREAD PUDDING

Reuben Bread Pudding

Our Aunt Renee always brought this casserole to our family picnics in Chicago. It became so popular that she started bringing two or three. I have also used dark rye bread or marbled rye, and ham instead of corned beef.

—JOHNNA JOHNSON SCOTTSDALE, AZ

PREP: 20 MIN. • **BAKE:** 35 MIN.
MAKES: 6 SERVINGS

- 4 **cups cubed rye bread (about 6 slices)**
- 2 **tablespoons butter, melted**
- 2 **cups cubed or shredded cooked corned beef (about ½ pound)**
- 1 **can (14 ounces) sauerkraut, rinsed and well drained**
- 1 **cup (4 ounces) shredded Swiss cheese, divided**
- 3 **eggs**
- 1 **cup 2% milk**
- ⅓ **cup prepared Thousand Island salad dressing**
- 1½ **teaspoons prepared mustard**
- ¼ **teaspoon pepper**

1. Preheat oven to 350°. In a large bowl, toss bread cubes with butter. Stir in corned beef, sauerkraut and ½ cup cheese; transfer to a greased 11x7-in. baking dish.
2. In the same bowl, whisk the eggs, milk, salad dressing, mustard and pepper; pour over top. Bake, uncovered, 30 minutes. Sprinkle with the remaining cheese. Bake 5-7 minutes longer or until golden and a knife inserted near the center comes out clean.

Short Rib Cobbler

This recipe was inspired by my family's love of two things—beef stew and biscuits. After years of making the two separately, I put the biscuits on top of the stew like a cobbler. This supper's as down-home good as it gets.

—JANINE TALLEY ORLANDO, FL

PREP: 45 MIN. • **BAKE:** 3 HOURS
MAKES: 8 SERVINGS

- ½ **cup plus 3 tablespoons all-purpose flour, divided**
- 1¼ **teaspoons salt, divided**
- ½ **teaspoon pepper**
- 2 **pounds well-trimmed boneless beef short ribs, cut into 1½-in. pieces**
- 5 **tablespoons olive oil, divided**
- 1 **large onion, chopped**
- 1 **medium carrot, chopped**
- 1 **celery rib, chopped**
- 1 **garlic clove, minced**
- 2 **tablespoons tomato paste**
- 5 **cups beef stock**
- 1 **cup dry red wine or additional beef stock**
- 1 **teaspoon poultry seasoning**
- 1 **bay leaf**
- 1 **package (14 ounces) frozen pearl onions, thawed**
- 4 **medium carrots, cut into 2-inch pieces**

COBBLER TOPPING
- 2 **cups biscuit/baking mix**
- ⅔ **cup 2% milk**
  Fresh thyme leaves

1. Preheat oven to 350°. In a shallow bowl, mix ½ cup flour, ¾ teaspoon salt and pepper. Dip short ribs in the flour mixture to coat all sides; shake off excess.
2. In an ovenproof Dutch oven, heat 3 tablespoons oil over medium heat. Brown beef in batches. Remove from the pan.
3. In the same pan, heat remaining oil over medium heat. Add onion, chopped carrot and celery; cook and stir 2-3 minutes or until tender. Add garlic; cook 1 minute longer. Stir in tomato paste and remaining flour until blended. Gradually stir in stock and wine until smooth. Return beef to pan; stir in poultry seasoning, bay leaf and remaining salt. Bring to a boil.
4. Bake, covered, 1¾ hours. Stir in pearl onions and carrot pieces. Bake, covered, 30-45 minutes longer or until beef and onions are tender. Skim fat and remove bay leaf.
5. In a small bowl, mix biscuit mix and milk just until a soft dough forms. Drop by scant ¼ cupfuls over beef mixture. Bake, uncovered, 40-45 minutes longer or until topping is golden brown. Sprinkle with thyme.

Pizza Mac & Cheese

My grandchildren love this upgraded macaroni and cheese. Adding ground beef, pizza fixings and shredded cheese makes quite an impressive meal out of a mix that comes from a box.

—**NANCY PORTERFIELD** GAP MILLS, WV

PREP: 30 MIN. • **BAKE:** 30 MIN.
MAKES: 6 SERVINGS

- 1 **package (7¼ ounces) macaroni and cheese dinner mix**
- 6 **cups water**
- 1 **pound ground beef**
- 1 **medium onion, chopped**
- 1 **small green pepper, chopped**
- 1½ **cups (6 ounces) shredded part-skim mozzarella cheese, divided**
- 1½ **cups (6 ounces) shredded cheddar cheese, divided**
- 1 **jar (14 ounces) pizza sauce**
- ½ **cup sliced pepperoni**

1. Set the cheese packet from dinner mix aside. In a saucepan, bring water to a boil. Add macaroni; cook for 8-10 minutes or until tender.

2. Meanwhile, in a large skillet, cook the beef, onion and green pepper over medium heat until meat is no longer pink; drain.

3. Drain macaroni; stir in contents of cheese packet. Transfer to a greased round 2½-qt. baking dish. Sprinkle with ½ cup mozzarella cheese and ½ cup cheddar cheese. Top with the beef mixture, pizza sauce, pepperoni and remaining cheeses.

4. Bake, uncovered, at 350° for 30-35 minutes or until heated through.

Roast Beef with Chive Roasted Potatoes

It's hard to believe that last night's beef roast could get any better, but it shines in this heartwarming dish.

—*TASTE OF HOME* **TEST KITCHEN**

PREP: 20 MIN. • **BAKE:** 25 MIN.
MAKES: 6 SERVINGS

- 2 **pounds red potatoes, cut into 1-inch cubes**
- 2 **tablespoons olive oil**
- 2 **teaspoons minced chives**
- ¾ **teaspoon salt, divided**
- 2 **medium onions, halved and thinly sliced**
- 1 **pound sliced fresh mushrooms**
- ¼ **cup butter, cubed**
- 1 **garlic clove, minced**
- 1 **teaspoon dried rosemary, crushed**
- ¼ **teaspoon pepper**
- ⅓ **cup dry red wine or beef broth**
- 2 **cups cubed cooked roast beef**
- 1 **cup beef gravy**

1. Place potatoes in a greased 15x10x1-in. baking pan. Drizzle with oil and sprinkle with chives and ¼ teaspoon salt; toss to coat. Bake, uncovered, at 425° for 25-30 minutes or until tender, stirring occasionally.

2. Meanwhile, in a large skillet, saute onions and mushrooms in butter until tender. Add the garlic, rosemary, pepper and remaining salt; cook 1 minute longer. Stir in wine. Add beef and gravy; heat through. Serve with the potatoes.

Three-Cheese Jumbo Shells

I love cooking, but I'm not into fancy gourmet foods. I think it's more of a fun challenge to make delicious, comforting meals with ingredients easily found in the refrigerator and on my pantry shelves.
—MARJORIE CAREY ALAMOSA, CO

PREP: 45 MIN. • **BAKE:** 35 MIN.
MAKES: 6-8 SERVINGS

- 1 pound ground beef
- ⅔ cup chopped onion
- 2 cups water
- 2 cans (6 ounces each) tomato paste
- 1 tablespoon beef bouillon granules
- 1½ teaspoons dried oregano
- 1 carton (15 ounces) ricotta cheese
- 2 cups (8 ounces) shredded part-skim mozzarella cheese, divided
- ½ cup grated Parmesan cheese
- 1 egg, lightly beaten
- 24 jumbo pasta shells, cooked and drained

1. In a large skillet, cook beef and onion over medium heat until the meat is no longer pink; drain. Stir in water, tomato paste, bouillon and oregano. Cover and simmer for 30 minutes.

2. Meanwhile, in a large bowl, combine the ricotta cheese, 1 cup mozzarella, Parmesan cheese and egg. Stuff shells with the cheese mixture.

3. Arrange shells in a greased shallow 3-qt. baking dish. Spoon meat sauce over shells. Cover and bake at 350° for 30 minutes. Uncover; sprinkle with remaining mozzarella cheese. Bake 3-5 minutes longer or until the cheese is melted.

Sloppy Joe Veggie Casserole

Sloppy joe flavor meets veggie lasagna wholesomeness in one pan. My family loves this dynamic duo, and you'll love how simple it is to prepare.
—SUE SCHMIDTKE ORO VALLEY, AZ

PREP: 25 MIN. • **BAKE:** 30 MIN.
MAKES: 8 SERVINGS

- 2½ cups uncooked penne pasta
- 1 pound ground beef
- 1 small onion, chopped

- 1 package (16 ounces) frozen mixed vegetables
- 1½ cups water
- 1 can (15 ounces) tomato sauce
- 1 can (6 ounces) tomato paste
- 1 envelope sloppy joe mix
- 1 tablespoon dried parsley flakes
- ½ teaspoon dried oregano
- 2 cups (16 ounces) 2% cottage cheese
- 1½ cups (6 ounces) shredded Colby-Monterey Jack cheese, divided

1. Cook pasta according to package directions.

2. Meanwhile, cook beef and onion in a large skillet over medium heat until meat is no longer pink; drain. Add the vegetables, water, tomato sauce, tomato paste, sloppy joe mix, parsley and oregano. Bring to a boil. Reduce heat; simmer, uncovered, for 7-9 minutes or until vegetables are crisp-tender. Drain pasta; stir into beef mixture. Spoon half of the mixture into a greased 13x9-in. baking dish. Top with cottage cheese, ¾ cup Colby-Monterey Jack and remaining pasta mixture. Cover and bake at 350° for 25 minutes. Uncover; sprinkle with remaining Colby-Monterey Jack cheese. Bake 5-10 minutes longer or until bubbly and cheese is melted.

THREE-CHEESE JUMBO SHELLS

Sicilian Supper

Ground beef, tomato and a tasty cream cheese sauce come together in this hot, savory casserole. I recently took it to a banquet, and recipe requests came from every table.

—**GLORIA WARCZAK** CEDARBURG, WI

PREP: 30 MIN. • **BAKE:** 20 MIN.
MAKES: 4 SERVINGS

- 2 cups uncooked egg noodles
- 1 pound ground beef
- ½ cup chopped onion
- ¼ cup chopped green pepper
- 1 can (6 ounces) tomato paste
- ¾ cup water
- 1½ teaspoons sugar, divided
- ½ teaspoon salt
- ½ teaspoon dried basil
- ¼ teaspoon garlic powder
- ¼ teaspoon chili powder
- ¼ teaspoon pepper, divided
- 1 tablespoon finely chopped green onion
- 1 tablespoon olive oil
- 1 package (8 ounces) cream cheese, cubed
- ¾ cup milk
- ⅓ cup plus 2 tablespoons grated Parmesan cheese, divided

1. Preheat oven to 350°. Cook noodles according to package directions.
2. Meanwhile, in a large skillet, cook beef, onion and green pepper over medium heat until meat is no longer pink; drain. Stir in tomato paste, water, 1 teaspoon sugar, salt, basil, garlic powder, chili powder and ⅛ teaspoon pepper.
3. In a large saucepan, saute green onion in oil until tender. Add cream cheese and milk; stir until blended. Stir in ⅓ cup cheese and remaining sugar and pepper. Drain noodles; stir into cheese mixture.
4. In a greased 8-in.-square baking dish, arrange alternate rows of beef and noodle mixtures. Sprinkle with remaining cheese. Cover and bake 20-25 minutes or until bubbly.

Mexican Beef Cobbler

Add whatever you like to this satisfying Mexican cobbler to make it your own— black beans, chipotle peppers in adobo sauce, sour cream or even guacamole!

—**MARY BROOKS** CLAY, MI

PREP: 20 MIN. • **BAKE:** 35 MIN.
MAKES: 6 SERVINGS

- 1½ pounds ground beef
- 1 envelope taco seasoning
- 1 jar (16 ounces) salsa
- 1 can (8¾ ounces) whole kernel corn, drained
- 2 cups (8 ounces) shredded sharp cheddar cheese
- 1½ cups biscuit/baking mix
- ½ cup 2% milk
- ⅛ teaspoon freshly ground pepper

1. In a large skillet, cook beef over medium heat for 8-10 minutes or until no longer pink, breaking into crumbles; drain. Stir in taco seasoning, salsa and corn; heat through. Transfer to an 11x7-in. baking dish; sprinkle with cheese.
2. In a small bowl, mix biscuit mix and milk just until blended; drop by tablespoonfuls over cheese. Sprinkle with pepper.
3. Bake, uncovered, at 350° for 35-45 minutes or until bubbly and topping is golden brown.

Quick Shepherd's Pie

Shepherd's pie is great with leftover homemade mashed potatoes, but it's just as good with ready-made mashed potatoes from the grocery store, too.

—**JENNIFER EARLY** EAST LANSING, MI

START TO FINISH: 20 MIN.
MAKES: 4 SERVINGS

- 1 tub (24 ounces) refrigerated cheddar mashed potatoes
- 1 pound lean ground beef (90% lean)
- 1 envelope mushroom gravy mix
- 1½ cups frozen mixed vegetables
- 1 cup water
- ⅛ teaspoon pepper

1. Heat potatoes according to package directions.
2. Meanwhile, in a large skillet, cook the beef over medium heat for 6-8 minutes or until no longer pink, breaking into crumbles; drain. Stir in gravy mix. Add vegetables and water; bring to boil. Reduce heat; simmer until heated through, stirring occasionally. Transfer to a 9-in.-square baking pan.
3. Spread the potatoes over top; sprinkle with pepper. Broil 4-6 in. from the heat for 10-15 minutes or until golden brown.

MEXICAN BEEF COBBLER

GILDA LESTER'S TURKEY & SPINACH STUFFING CASSEROLE *PAGE 39*

Poultry

READY TO INTRODUCE A NEW FAVORITE AT YOUR NEXT MEAL?
YOUR FAMILY WILL DIG INTO THESE ONE-DISH WONDERS.

LEMONY CHICKEN & RICE

Lemony Chicken & Rice

I couldn't say who loves this recipe most, because every time I serve it, it gets raves. It's certainly a favorite of my grown children and 15 grandchildren.
—**MARYALICE ANN WOOD** LANGLEY, BC

PREP: 15 MIN. + MARINATING
BAKE: 55 MIN.
MAKES: 2 CASSEROLES (4 SERVINGS EACH)

- 2 **cups water**
- ½ **cup reduced-sodium soy sauce**
- ¼ **cup lemon juice**
- ¼ **cup olive oil**
- 2 **garlic cloves, minced**
- 2 **teaspoons ground ginger**
- 2 **teaspoons pepper**
- 16 **bone-in chicken thighs, skin removed (about 6 pounds)**
- 2 **cups uncooked long grain rice**
- 4 **tablespoons grated lemon peel, divided**
- 2 **medium lemons, sliced**

1. In a large resealable plastic bag, combine the first seven ingredients. Add chicken; seal bag and turn to coat. Refrigerate 4 hours or overnight.

2. Preheat the oven to 325°. Spread 1 cup rice into each of two greased 13x9-in. baking dishes. Top each with 1 tablespoon lemon peel, 8 chicken thighs and half of the marinade. Top with sliced lemons.

3. Bake, covered, 40 minutes. Bake, uncovered, 15-20 minutes longer or until a thermometer inserted in chicken reads 180°. Sprinkle with remaining lemon peel.

DID YOU KNOW?

Long grain rice and instant rice (which is precooked before packaging) require different amounts of liquid during cooking, so they cannot be substituted measure for measure in recipes that call for uncooked rice (like Lemony Chicken & Rice). However, if a recipe calls for cooked rice, you can use either kind interchangeably.

Spinach Chicken Casserole

I came up with this based on a recipe I found on a spaghetti sauce label, with a few substitutions and additions here and there. I was quite pleased with the results!

—**JACKIE WOOD** JACKSON, TN

PREP: 20 MIN. • **BAKE:** 20 MIN.
MAKES: 6 SERVINGS

- 2 cups uncooked penne pasta
- ¾ pound boneless skinless chicken breasts, cubed
- 1 small onion, chopped
- ½ cup chopped green pepper
- 1 jar (26 ounces) spaghetti sauce
- 1 package (16 ounces) frozen leaf spinach, thawed and squeezed dry
- 1 jar (6 ounces) sliced mushrooms, drained
- 1 can (2¼ ounces) sliced ripe olives, drained
- 2 cups (8 ounces) shredded part-skim mozzarella cheese, divided

1. Cook pasta according to package directions. Meanwhile, in a large nonstick saucepan coated with cooking spray, saute chicken until no longer pink; set aside.
2. In the same pan, saute onion and green pepper until crisp-tender. Add spaghetti sauce, spinach, mushrooms and olives. Bring to a boil. Reduce heat; simmer, uncovered, for 5 minutes. Drain pasta; add chicken and pasta to the pan. Sprinkle with 1 cup cheese and toss to coat.
3. Transfer to a 13x9-in. baking dish coated with cooking spray; sprinkle with remaining cheese. Cover and bake at 350° for 20-25 minutes or until cheese is melted.

Chicken Taco Pie

This family fave comes to the rescue on busy nights when we've been rushing to soccer, swimming lessons or Scouts. I put it together in the morning and just pop it in the oven when we get home.

—**KAREN LATIMER** WINNIPEG, MB

PREP: 20 MIN. • **BAKE:** 30 MIN.
MAKES: 6 SERVINGS

- 1 tube (8 ounces) refrigerated crescent rolls
- 1 pound ground chicken
- 1 envelope taco seasoning
- 1 can (4 ounces) chopped green chilies
- ½ cup water
- ½ cup salsa
- ½ cup shredded Mexican cheese blend
- 1 cup shredded lettuce
- 1 small sweet red pepper, chopped
- 1 small green pepper, chopped
- 1 medium tomato, seeded and chopped
- 1 green onion, thinly sliced
- 2 tablespoons pickled jalapeno slices
  Sour cream and additional salsa

1. Preheat oven to 350°. Unroll crescent dough and separate into triangles. Press onto bottom of a greased 9-in. pie plate to form a crust, sealing seams well. Bake 18-20 minutes or until golden brown.
2. Meanwhile, in a large skillet, cook chicken over medium heat 6-8 minutes or until no longer pink, breaking into crumbles; drain. Stir in taco seasoning, green chilies, water and salsa; bring to a boil.
3. Spoon into crust; sprinkle with cheese. Bake 8-10 minutes or until cheese is melted.
4. Top with the lettuce, peppers, tomato, green onion and pickled jalapeno. Serve with sour cream and additional salsa.

CHICKEN TACO PIE

PORTOBELLO
PASTA BAKE

Chicken Pie in a Pan

It takes a little extra time to prepare this potpie, but luckily I have five children at home to lend a hand. This dish travels well, so it's the ideal thing to bring along to a potluck or family reunion.

—KRISTINE CONWAY ALLIANCE, OH

PREP: 25 MIN. • **BAKE:** 35 MIN.
MAKES: 6-8 SERVINGS

- 2 celery ribs, diced
- 2 medium carrots, diced
- 1 small onion, chopped
- 3 tablespoons butter
- ¼ cup all-purpose flour
- ½ teaspoon salt
- 1 cup 2% milk
- 1 cup chicken broth
- 1 can (10¾ ounces) condensed cream of mushroom soup, undiluted
- 4 cups cubed cooked chicken

CRUST
- 1½ cups all-purpose flour
- ¾ teaspoon baking powder
- 1 teaspoon salt
- 3 tablespoons cold butter
- ½ cup 2% milk
- 2 cups (8 ounces) shredded cheddar cheese

1. In a large skillet, saute the celery, carrots and onion in butter until tender. Stir in flour and salt until blended; gradually add milk and broth. Bring to a boil; cook and stir for 2 minutes or until thickened. Stir in soup and chicken. Spoon into a greased 13x9-in. baking dish; set aside.
2. For crust, combine flour, baking powder and salt. Cut in butter until crumbly. Add milk, tossing with a fork until mixture forms a soft dough; shape into a ball.
3. On a lightly floured surface, roll into a 12x10-in. rectangle. Sprinkle with cheese. Roll up jelly-roll style, starting from a long side. Cut into 12 slices. Place cut side down over chicken mixture. Bake, uncovered, at 350° for 35-40 minutes or until the crust is lightly browned.

Portobello Pasta Bake

Have extra turkey after a big meal or holiday? Your leftovers will be dressed to impress in this satisfying casserole.

—PRECI D'SILVA DUBAI, UAE

PREP: 20 MIN. • **BAKE:** 20 MIN.
MAKES: 4 SERVINGS

- 2½ cups uncooked multigrain spiral pasta
- 3 large portobello mushrooms
- 1 tablespoon olive oil
- 1 tablespoon butter
- 3 garlic cloves, minced
- 3 tablespoons all-purpose flour
- 1½ cups 2% milk
- ⅓ cup heavy whipping cream
- 2 cups cubed cooked turkey
- ¾ teaspoon salt
- ¼ teaspoon pepper
- 1 cup (4 ounces) shredded part-skim mozzarella cheese, divided
- 2 tablespoons grated Parmesan cheese

1. Preheat oven to 350°. Cook pasta according to package directions. With a spoon, scrape and remove gills of mushrooms; slice caps.
2. In a large skillet, heat oil and butter over medium-high heat. Add sliced mushrooms; cook and stir until tender. Add garlic; cook 1 minute longer. Stir in flour until blended; gradually add milk and cream. Bring to a boil; cook and stir 2 minutes or until thickened. Stir in turkey, salt and pepper; heat through.
3. Drain pasta; add to the turkey mixture and toss to coat. Stir in ¾ cup mozzarella cheese.
4. Transfer to a greased 8-in.-square baking dish. Sprinkle with Parmesan cheese and remaining mozzarella cheese. Bake, uncovered, 20-25 minutes or until cheese is melted.

Mexicali Casserole

Kids gobble up this Mexican-style supper. It's mild enough for the little ones and seasoned enough for everyone else.
—GERTRUDIS MILLER EVANSVILLE, IN

PREP: 15 MIN. • **BAKE:** 55 MIN.
MAKES: 6 SERVINGS

- 1 **pound lean ground turkey**
- 2 **medium onions, chopped**
- 1 **small green pepper, chopped**
- 1 **garlic clove, minced**
- 1 **can (16 ounces) kidney beans, rinsed and drained**
- 1 **can (14½ ounces) diced tomatoes, undrained**
- 1 **cup water**
- ⅔ **cup uncooked long grain rice**
- ⅓ **cup sliced ripe olives**
- 1 **teaspoon chili powder**
- ½ **teaspoon salt**
- ½ **cup shredded reduced-fat cheddar cheese**

1. Preheat oven to 375°. In a large skillet coated with cooking spray, cook turkey, onions and pepper over medium heat 6-8 minutes or until meat is no longer pink and vegetables are tender, breaking up turkey into crumbles. Add garlic; cook 1 minute longer. Drain. Stir in the beans, tomatoes, water, rice, olives, chili powder and salt.

2. Transfer to an 11x7-in. baking dish coated with cooking spray. Bake, covered, 50-55 minutes or until rice is tender. Sprinkle with cheese. Bake, uncovered, 5 minutes longer or until cheese is melted.

Country Chicken Casserole

Whenever I make this entree, someone asks for the recipe. Best of all, you can fix it ahead to simplify your mealtime prep.
—SUE KENNEDY GALLOWAY, OH

PREP: 45 MIN. + CHILLING
BAKE: 45 MIN. + STANDING
MAKES: 8 SERVINGS

- 1 **package (6 ounces) Stove Top chicken stuffing mix**
- ½ **pound sliced fresh mushrooms**
- 1 **small onion, chopped**
- 1 **tablespoon butter**
- 3 **garlic cloves, minced**
- 3 **cups cubed cooked chicken**
- 1 **package (16 ounces) frozen corn, thawed**
- 1 **package (16 ounces) frozen chopped broccoli, thawed**
- 1 **can (10¾ ounces) reduced-fat reduced-sodium condensed cream of mushroom soup, undiluted**
- 1 **cup 2% milk**
- 1 **cup reduced-fat sour cream**
- 1 **cup reduced-fat mayonnaise**
- ¾ **teaspoon pepper**

1. Prepare stuffing according to package directions. Meanwhile, in a large skillet, saute mushrooms and onion in butter until tender. Add garlic; cook 1 minute longer.

2. In a large bowl, combine chicken, corn, broccoli, soup, milk, sour cream, mayonnaise, pepper and mushroom mixture; transfer to a greased 13x9-in. baking dish. Top with stuffing. Cover and refrigerate overnight.

3. Remove from the refrigerator 30 minutes before baking. Cover and bake at 350° for 35 minutes. Uncover and bake 10-15 minutes longer or until stuffing is lightly browned. Let stand for 10 minutes before serving.

MEXICALI CASSEROLE

Chicken Spaghetti Casserole

I first made this meal when I had unexpected guests. It's a lifesaver when I'm in a hurry because it takes only minutes to assemble.

—BERNICE JANOWSKI STEVENS POINT, WI

PREP: 20 MIN. • **BAKE:** 40 MIN.
MAKES: 4 SERVINGS

- 8 ounces uncooked spaghetti
- 1 cup ricotta cheese
- 1 cup (4 ounces) shredded part-skim mozzarella cheese, divided
- 2 tablespoons grated Parmesan cheese
- ½ teaspoon Italian seasoning
- ½ teaspoon garlic powder
- 1 jar (26 ounces) meatless spaghetti sauce
- 1 can (14½ ounces) Italian diced tomatoes, undrained
- 1 jar (4½ ounces) sliced mushrooms, drained
- 4 breaded fully cooked chicken patties (10 to 14 ounces)

1. Cook spaghetti according to package directions. Meanwhile, in a large bowl, combine ricotta, ½ cup of mozzarella, Parmesan, Italian seasoning and garlic powder; set aside. In another bowl, combine spaghetti sauce, tomatoes and mushrooms.
2. Drain spaghetti; add 2 cups spaghetti sauce mixture and toss to coat. Transfer to a greased 13x9-in. baking dish; top with cheese mixture.
3. Arrange chicken patties over the top; drizzle with the remaining spaghetti sauce mixture. Sprinkle with the remaining mozzarella. Bake, uncovered, at 350° for 40-45 minutes or until bubbly.

MOM'S TURKEY TETRAZZINI

Mom's Turkey Tetrazzini

Full of family-friendly flavors, a pleasant peppery kick and made-from-scratch sauce, this hearty dish is just the dinner you've been looking for.

—JUDY BATSON TAMPA, FL

PREP: 25 MIN. • **BAKE:** 25 MIN. + STANDING
MAKES: 6 SERVINGS

- 1 package (12 ounces) fettuccine
- ½ pound sliced fresh mushrooms
- 1 medium onion, chopped
- ¼ cup butter, cubed
- 3 tablespoons all-purpose flour
- 3 cups 2% milk
- 1 cup white wine or chicken broth
- 3 cups cubed cooked turkey
- ¾ teaspoon salt
- ½ teaspoon pepper
- ½ teaspoon hot pepper sauce
- ½ cup shredded Parmesan cheese
  Paprika, optional

1. Preheat oven to 375°. Cook fettuccine according to package directions.
2. Meanwhile, in a large skillet, saute mushrooms and onion in butter until tender. Stir in flour until blended; gradually add milk and wine. Bring to a boil; cook and stir 2 minutes or until thickened. Stir in turkey, salt, pepper and pepper sauce.
3. Drain fettuccine. Layer half of the fettuccine, turkey mixture and cheese in a greased 13x9-in. baking dish. Repeat layers. Sprinkle with paprika if desired.
4. Cover and bake 25-30 minutes or until heated through. Let stand 10 minutes before serving.

Southwest-Style Shepherd's Pie

I was born in Montreal and lived in the Southwest before moving to New England, so I've merged these influences into recipes like this casserole with turkey, corn and green chilies.
—**LYNN PRICE** MILLVILLE, MA

PREP: 20 MIN. • **BAKE:** 25 MIN.
MAKES: 6 SERVINGS

- 1¼ **pounds lean ground turkey**
- 1 **small onion, chopped**
- 2 **garlic cloves, minced**
- ½ **teaspoon salt, divided**
- 1 **can (14¾ ounces) cream-style corn**
- 1 **can (4 ounces) chopped green chilies**
- 1 **to 2 tablespoons chipotle hot pepper sauce, optional**
- 2⅔ **cups water**
- 2 **tablespoons butter**
- 2 **tablespoons half-and-half cream**
- ½ **teaspoon pepper**
- 2 **cups mashed potato flakes**

1. Preheat oven to 425°. In a large skillet, cook turkey, onion, garlic and ¼ teaspoon salt over medium heat 8-10 minutes or until turkey is no longer pink and onion is tender, breaking up turkey into crumbles. Stir in corn, green chilies and, if desired, pepper sauce. Transfer to a greased 8-in.-square baking dish.

2. Meanwhile, in a saucepan, bring water, butter, cream, pepper and remaining salt to a boil. Remove from heat. Stir in potato flakes. Spoon over turkey mixture, spreading to cover. Bake 25-30 minutes or until bubbly and potatoes are light brown.

Chicken and Olive Mole Casserole

My spiced-up casserole makes the ideal party dish when you're looking for something a little out of the ordinary. The mole sauce lends an authentic Mexican flavor, and folks are always pleasantly surprised to taste a little sweetness from the chocolate.

—BARBARA WHITE LIVINGSTON, TX

PREP: 50 MIN. • **BAKE:** 40 MIN. + STANDING
MAKES: 8 SERVINGS

- 2 large onions, finely chopped, divided
- 3 tablespoons olive oil
- 3 garlic cloves, minced
- 1 teaspoon salt
- 1 teaspoon dried oregano
- 1 teaspoon ground cumin
- ¼ teaspoon ground cinnamon
- 5 tablespoons chili powder
- 3 tablespoons all-purpose flour
- 4½ cups reduced-sodium chicken broth
- ½ ounce semisweet chocolate, coarsely chopped
- 6 cups shredded cooked chicken
- 12 corn tortillas (6 inches), warmed
- 1 cup sliced pimiento-stuffed olives
- 4 cups (16 ounces) shredded Monterey Jack cheese

1. In a large saucepan, saute 1 cup onion in oil until tender. Reduce heat to low. Add the garlic, salt, oregano, cumin and cinnamon; cover and cook for 10 minutes. Stir in chili powder and flour until blended. Gradually stir in broth. Bring to a boil. Cook until mixture is reduced to 3 cups, about 35 minutes. Remove from the heat; stir in chocolate.

2. In a large bowl, combine chicken and ½ cup sauce mixture. Spread ½ cup sauce mixture into a greased 13x9-in. baking dish. Layer with half of the tortillas, chicken mixture, remaining onion and olives; top with 1 cup sauce and 2 cups cheese. Repeat the layers.

3. Cover and bake at 375° for 30 minutes. Uncover; bake 10-15 minutes longer or until cheese is melted. Let stand for 10 minutes before serving.

TOP TIP

Mole sauce is used in traditional Mexican dishes. It is a rich, brown sauce made with a variety of chili peppers, onion, garlic and chocolate.

CHICKEN AND OLIVE
MOLE CASSEROLE

Buffalo Chicken Pasta Bake

Sure, 10-cent wing night at your local pub is a blast, but a night at home with this clever casserole can't be beat. If you're not fond of blue cheese, use ranch salad dressing instead.

—**LINDSAY SPRUNK** NOBLESVILLE, IN

PREP: 30 MIN. • **BAKE:** 25 MIN.
MAKES: 8 SERVINGS

- 1 package (16 ounces) penne pasta
- 1 pound boneless skinless chicken breasts, cubed
- ⅛ teaspoon salt
- ⅛ teaspoon pepper
- 2 tablespoons olive oil, divided
- 2 medium carrots, finely chopped
- 2 celery ribs, finely chopped
- ¾ cup finely chopped red onion
- 4 garlic cloves, minced
- ¾ cup blue cheese salad dressing
- ¾ cup mayonnaise
- ½ cup Louisiana-style hot sauce
- 1½ cups (6 ounces) shredded Swiss cheese
- ½ cup dry bread crumbs
- 3 tablespoons butter, melted

1. Cook pasta according to package directions.

2. Meanwhile, sprinkle chicken with salt and pepper. In a large skillet, saute chicken in 1 tablespoon oil until no longer pink. Remove from skillet. In the same skillet, saute carrots, celery and onion in remaining oil until tender. Add garlic; cook 1 minute longer. Remove from heat.

3. Preheat oven to 350°. Stir salad dressing, mayonnaise and hot sauce into skillet. Drain pasta. Add pasta and chicken to skillet; toss to coat. Transfer to a greased 13x9-in. baking dish. Sprinkle with cheese and bread crumbs. Drizzle with butter.

4. Bake, uncovered, 25-30 minutes or until heated through and cheese is melted.

Chicken & Egg Noodle Casserole

After a fire at my friend's house, my heart broke for Michelle and her family. Bringing over this casserole was the one thing I could think of to help her out in a tiny way and let her know I was thinking of her and her family.

—**LIN KRANKEL** OXFORD, MI

PREP: 20 MIN. • **BAKE:** 30 MIN.
MAKES: 8 SERVINGS

- 6 cups uncooked egg noodles (about 12 ounces)
- 2 cans (10¾ ounces each) condensed cream of chicken soup, undiluted
- 1 cup (8 ounces) sour cream
- ¾ cup 2% milk
- ¼ teaspoon salt
- ¼ teaspoon pepper
- 3 cups cubed cooked chicken breasts
- 1 cup crushed butter-flavored crackers (about 20 crackers)
- ¼ cup butter, melted

1. Preheat oven to 350°. Cook noodles according to package directions for al dente; drain.

2. In a large bowl, whisk the soup, sour cream, milk, salt and pepper until blended. Stir in the chicken and noodles. Transfer to a greased 13x9-in. baking dish. In a small bowl, mix crushed crackers and butter; sprinkle over top. Bake 30-35 minutes or until bubbly.

CHICKEN & EGG
NOODLE CASSEROLE

CURRIED CHICKEN AND GRITS CASSEROLE

Curried Chicken and Grits Casserole

I moved to the South about seven years ago from Ohio. I've been creating recipes with grits recently and feel like I'm finally getting the Southern vibe! This casserole turns out beautifully with the mix of veggies, golden sauce and cheese-crusted grits on top.

—LORI SHAMSZADEH FAIRHOPE, AL

PREP: 25 MIN. • **BAKE:** 50 MIN.
MAKES: 8 SERVINGS

- 1 cup water
- 1½ cups chicken broth, divided
- ¼ teaspoon salt
- ½ cup quick-cooking grits
- 2 large eggs, beaten
- 2 cups (8 ounces) shredded cheddar cheese, divided
- 3 tablespoons butter, cubed
- 1 can (10¾ ounces) condensed cream of chicken and mushroom soup, undiluted
- 1½ cups mayonnaise
- 2 teaspoons curry powder
- 1 package (16 ounces) frozen broccoli-cauliflower blend
- 2 cups cubed cooked chicken
- 2 cups refrigerated diced potatoes with onion

1. Bring water, 1 cup broth and salt to a boil in a large saucepan. Slowly stir in grits. Reduce heat; cook and stir 5-6 minutes or until thickened.

Remove from heat; stir a small amount of grits into eggs. Return all to pan, stirring constantly. Add 1½ cups cheese and butter; stir until melted.
2. Preheat oven to 350°. Combine soup, mayonnaise, curry powder and remaining broth in a large bowl. Add vegetable blend, chicken and potatoes; toss to coat. Transfer to a greased 13x9-in. baking dish. Top with grits; sprinkle with remaining cheese.
3. Bake, uncovered, 50-55 minutes or until heated through.

FREEZE IT
Chicken Alfredo Stuffed Shells

These pasta shells, filled with warm, gooey cheese, are always a hit. The tender chicken and rich sauce make the dish so hearty, I simply serve salad on the side.

—MICHELE SHEPPARD MASONTOWN, PA

PREP: 45 MIN. • **BAKE:** 40 MIN.
MAKES: 10 SERVINGS

- 1 package (12 ounces) jumbo pasta shells
- 1½ pounds boneless skinless chicken breasts, cut into ½-inch cubes
- 2 tablespoons olive oil, divided
- ½ pound sliced baby portobello mushrooms
- 1 large egg, lightly beaten
- 1 carton (15 ounces) ricotta cheese
- 3¾ cups grated Parmesan cheese, divided
- 1 cup (4 ounces) shredded part-skim mozzarella cheese
- 1 teaspoon dried parsley flakes
- ¾ teaspoon salt
- ½ teaspoon pepper
- ½ cup butter, cubed
- 2 garlic cloves, minced
- 2 cups heavy whipping cream

1. Cook pasta according to package directions.
2. Meanwhile, in a large skillet, brown chicken in 1 tablespoon oil. Remove and set aside. In the same pan, saute mushrooms in remaining oil until tender; set aside. In a small bowl, combine the egg, ricotta, 1½ cups Parmesan, mozzarella and seasonings.
3. Drain and rinse pasta with cold water; stuff each shell with about 1 tablespoon of cheese mixture. Place in a greased 13x9-in. baking dish. Top with chicken and mushrooms.
4. In a large saucepan over medium heat, melt butter. Add garlic; cook and stir for 1 minute. Add cream; cook 5 minutes longer. Add 1½ cups Parmesan cheese; cook and stir until thickened.
5. Pour sauce over the casserole. Sprinkle with remaining Parmesan cheese. Cover and bake at 350° for 30 minutes. Uncover; bake 10-15 minutes longer or until bubbly.
6. If desired, cover and freeze unbaked shells for up to 1 month.
TO USE FROZEN SHELLS *Thaw in the refrigerator. Let stand at room temperature for 30 minutes. Bake as directed.*

DID YOU KNOW?

When a recipe calls for grated Parmesan cheese, use the finely grated cheese sold in containers with shaker tops. If a recipe calls for shredded Parmesan, use the bagged shredded cheese found in the grocery store dairy section. If a baked or cooked recipe calls for grated and you have shredded on hand (or vice versa), you can usually sub in what you have with only a slight change in the final product.

Fontina Chicken & Pasta Bake

PREP: 25 MIN. • **BAKE:** 15 MIN.
MAKES: 2 CASSEROLES (4 SERVINGS EACH)

- 1 package (16 ounces) uncooked spiral pasta
- 4 teaspoons olive oil, divided
- 2 pounds boneless skinless chicken breasts, cut into ¾-inch cubes
- ½ pound sliced fresh mushrooms
- 4 garlic cloves, minced
- 3 cans (10¾ ounces each) condensed cream of mushroom soup, undiluted
- 1½ cups chicken broth
- 1½ cups (6 ounces) shredded fontina cheese, divided
- 4 teaspoons minced fresh oregano or 1¼ teaspoons dried oregano
- ½ teaspoon pepper
- 2 packages (6 ounces each) fresh baby spinach, coarsely chopped
- 2 medium tomatoes, chopped

1. Preheat oven to 350°. Cook pasta according to directions for al dente.
2. Meanwhile, heat 3 teaspoons oil in a Dutch oven over medium-high heat. Add chicken in batches; cook and stir 3-5 minutes or until no longer pink. Remove from pan.
3. In same pan, add mushrooms to remaining oil; cook and stir over medium-high heat 3-5 minutes or until tender. Add garlic; cook 1 minute longer. Stir in soup, broth, 1 cup cheese, oregano and pepper. Add spinach and tomatoes; return chicken to pan.
4. Drain pasta; add to soup mixture and toss to combine. Divide between two greased 8-in.-square baking dishes. Sprinkle with remaining cheese. Bake, covered, 15-20 minutes or until heated through.
FREEZE OPTION *Cool unbaked casseroles; cover and freeze. To use, partially thaw in refrigerator overnight. Remove from refrigerator 30 minutes before baking. Preheat oven to 350°. Cover casseroles with foil; bake as directed, increasing baking time to 1¼ hours or until heated through and a thermometer inserted in center reads 165°.*

This bake is so good, we adjusted the recipe to turn it into two casseroles. Eat one tonight and freeze one for later. It's awesome anytime! —*TASTE OF HOME* TEST KITCHEN

FONTINA CHICKEN & PASTA BAKE

SOUTHWESTERN TURKEY BAKE

¾ cup prepared pesto
⅔ cup heavy whipping cream
½ cup grated Parmesan cheese
½ cup dry bread crumbs
¼ cup butter, melted

1. Cook mostaccioli and chicken according to package directions. Meanwhile, in a large bowl, combine cheddar cheese, sour cream, ricotta, pesto, cream and Parmesan cheese.
2. Chop chicken tenders and drain mostaccioli; add to cheese mixture. Toss to coat. Transfer to two greased 11x7-in. baking dishes (dishes will be full). Combine bread crumbs and butter; sprinkle over the top.
3. Bake, uncovered, at 350° for 25-30 minutes or until golden brown.

Chicken Artichoke Casserole

With a flavor that's similar to artichoke dip, this robust chicken bake will warm you up on chilly nights.

—AMY NUTONI LA CRESCENT, MN

PREP: 20 MIN. • **BAKE:** 25 MIN.
MAKES: 6 SERVINGS

2 cups uncooked bow tie pasta
2 cups cubed cooked chicken
1 can (14 ounces) water-packed artichoke hearts, rinsed, drained and chopped
1 can (10¾ ounces) condensed cream of chicken soup, undiluted
1 cup shredded Parmesan cheese
1 cup mayonnaise
⅓ cup 2% milk
1 garlic clove, minced
½ teaspoon onion powder
½ teaspoon pepper
1 cup onion and garlic salad croutons, coarsely crushed

1. Preheat oven to 350°. Cook pasta according to package directions. Meanwhile, in a large bowl, combine chicken, artichokes, soup, cheese, mayonnaise, milk, garlic, onion powder and pepper. Drain pasta; add to chicken mixture.
2. Transfer to a greased 2-qt. baking dish. Sprinkle with croutons. Bake, uncovered, 25-30 minutes or until heated through.

Southwestern Turkey Bake

I make this as a way to get my nieces and husband to eat their vegetables. This entree will satisfy, too!

—CRYSTAL KOLADY HENRIETTA, NY

PREP: 20 MIN. • **BAKE:** 25 MIN.
MAKES: 12 SERVINGS

2 large onions, chopped
2 jalapeno peppers, seeded and chopped
2 tablespoons butter
6 cups cubed cooked turkey
2 cans (10¾ ounces each) condensed cream of chicken soup, undiluted
2 cups (16 ounces) sour cream
1 package (10 ounces) frozen chopped spinach, thawed and squeezed dry
2 cups (8 ounces) shredded Monterey Jack cheese
1 package (12½ ounces) nacho tortilla chips, crushed
4 green onions, sliced

1. Preheat the oven to 350°. In a Dutch oven, saute the onions and jalapenos in butter until tender. Stir in turkey, soup, sour cream and spinach.

In a greased 13x9-in. baking dish, layer half of the turkey mixture, cheese and tortilla chips. Repeat layers.
2. Bake, uncovered, 25-30 minutes or until bubbly. Let stand 5 minutes before serving. Sprinkle with the green onions.
NOTE *Wear disposable gloves when cutting hot peppers; the oils can burn skin. Avoid touching your face.*

Pesto Chicken Mostaccioli

I was looking for something new to whip up and decided to invent my own recipe. We love pesto and mac and cheese, but who knew what a yummy combination it would be with chicken nuggets! Comfort food to the max, this deliciously different casserole is great for a crowd.

—REBECCA STABLEIN LAKE FOREST, CA

PREP: 25 MIN. • **BAKE:** 25 MIN.
MAKES: 2 CASSEROLES (5 SERVINGS EACH)

1 package (16 ounces) mostaccioli
1 package (16 ounces) frozen breaded chicken tenders
4 cups (16 ounces) shredded cheddar cheese
1 container (16 ounces) sour cream
1 carton (15 ounces) ricotta cheese

Butternut Turkey Bake

FREEZE IT

Butternut squash adds a little sweetness to this unique turkey entree. You can use leftover meat and even replace the croutons with leftover stuffing. Expect your family to ask for seconds.

—MARY ANN DELL PHOENIXVILLE, PA

PREP: 70 MIN. • **BAKE:** 25 MIN.
MAKES: 4 SERVINGS

- 1 medium butternut squash (about 2½ pounds)
- ¾ cup finely chopped onion
- 2 tablespoons butter
- 2 cups seasoned salad croutons
- ½ teaspoon salt
- ½ teaspoon poultry seasoning
- ½ teaspoon pepper
- 2 cups cubed cooked turkey
- 1 cup chicken broth
- ½ cup shredded cheddar cheese

1. Cut the squash in half; discard seeds. Place cut side down in a 15x10x1-in. baking pan; add ½ in. of hot water. Bake, uncovered, at 350° for 45 minutes.

2. Drain water from pan; turn squash cut side up. Bake 10-15 minutes longer or until tender. Scoop out flesh; mash and set aside.

3. In a large skillet, saute onion in butter until tender. Stir in croutons, salt, poultry seasoning and pepper. Cook 2-3 minutes longer or until croutons are toasted. Stir in squash, turkey and broth; heat through.

4. Transfer to a greased 1½-qt. baking dish. Bake, uncovered, at 350° for 20 minutes. Sprinkle with cheese. Bake 5-10 minutes longer or until edges are bubbly and cheese is melted.

NOTE *Serve immediately or cover and freeze casserole for up to 3 months.*

TO USE FROZEN CASSEROLE *Remove from the freezer 30 minutes before baking (do not thaw). Cover and bake at 350° for 45-60 minutes. Uncover; bake 5-10 minutes longer or until edges are bubbly and cheese is melted.*

Chicken Amandine

With colorful green beans and pimientos, this attractive casserole is terrific for the holidays or family dinners. This is true down-home food.

—KAT WOOLBRIGHT WICHITA FALLS, TX

PREP: 35 MIN. • **BAKE:** 30 MIN.
MAKES: 8 SERVINGS

- ¼ cup chopped onion
- 1 tablespoon butter
- 1 package (6 ounces) long grain and wild rice
- 2¼ cups chicken broth
- 3 cups cubed cooked chicken
- 2 cups frozen French-style green beans, thawed
- 1 can (10¾ ounces) condensed cream of chicken soup, undiluted
- ¾ cup sliced almonds, divided
- 1 jar (4 ounces) diced pimientos, drained
- 1 teaspoon pepper
- ½ teaspoon garlic powder
- 1 bacon strip, cooked and crumbled

1. In a large saucepan, saute onion in butter until tender. Add rice with contents of seasoning packet and broth. Bring to a boil. Reduce heat; cover and simmer for 25 minutes or until liquid is absorbed. Uncover; set aside to cool.

2. In a large bowl, combine chicken, green beans, soup, ½ cup of almonds, pimientos, pepper and garlic powder. Stir in rice.

3. Transfer to a greased 2½-qt. baking dish. Sprinkle with bacon and remaining almonds. Cover and bake at 350° for 30-35 minutes or until heated through.

CHICKEN AMANDINE

Lattice-Topped Turkey Casserole

My friends tell me this is the best potpie. No one guesses that it's actually low in fat and high in fiber.

—AGNES WARD STRATFORD, ON

PREP: 45 MIN. • **BAKE:** 20 MIN. + STANDING
MAKES: 6 SERVINGS

- 1 can (14½ ounces) reduced-sodium chicken broth
- 2 cups diced red potatoes
- 2 celery ribs, chopped
- 1 large onion, finely chopped
- ½ cup water
- 2 teaspoons chicken bouillon granules
- ½ teaspoon dried rosemary, crushed
- ¼ teaspoon garlic powder
- ¼ teaspoon dried thyme
- ⅛ teaspoon pepper
- 3 tablespoons all-purpose flour
- ⅔ cup fat-free evaporated milk
- 3 cups frozen mixed vegetables, thawed and drained
- 2 cups cubed cooked turkey breast

CRUST

- ¼ cup all-purpose flour
- ¼ cup whole wheat flour
- ½ teaspoon baking powder
- ⅛ teaspoon salt
- 4 tablespoons fat-free milk, divided
- 1 tablespoon canola oil
  Paprika

1. In a large saucepan, combine first 10 ingredients. Bring to a boil. Reduce heat; cover and simmer for 15-20 minutes or until potatoes are tender.

2. In a small bowl, whisk flour and evaporated milk until smooth; stir into broth mixture. Bring to a boil; cook and stir for 2 minutes or until thickened. Stir in vegetables and turkey; heat through. Transfer to an ungreased 8-in.-square baking dish.

3. For crust, combine the flours, baking powder and salt in a small bowl. Stir in 3 tablespoons milk and oil just until combined. Roll out and cut into strips; make a lattice crust over filling. Trim and seal edges. Brush lattice top with remaining milk; sprinkle with paprika.

4. Bake, uncovered, at 400° for 20-25 minutes or until filling is bubbly. Let stand for 10 minutes before serving.

THREE-CHEESE & PEPPER PENNE

FREEZE IT

Three-Cheese & Pepper Penne

This cheesy pasta entree comes together in a snap. It makes two casseroles, so you can freeze one for later or share it with friends now.

—JASEY MCBURNETT ROCK SPRINGS, WY

PREP: 40 MIN. • **BAKE:** 30 MIN.
MAKES: 2 CASSEROLES (5 SERVINGS EACH)

- 1 package (16 ounces) penne pasta
- 1½ pounds boneless skinless chicken breasts, cut into ½-inch pieces
- 1¼ teaspoons salt
- ½ teaspoon pepper
- 3 teaspoons olive oil, divided
- 1 pound sliced fresh mushrooms
- 4 garlic cloves, minced
- ¼ cup butter, cubed
- ½ cup all-purpose flour
- 4 cups 2% milk
- 2 jars (7 ounces each) roasted sweet red peppers, drained and chopped
- 2 cups (8 ounces) shredded mozzarella and provolone cheese
- 2 cups grated Parmesan cheese, divided

1. Cook pasta according to package directions. Meanwhile, sprinkle chicken with salt and pepper. In a large skillet, saute the chicken in 1 teaspoon oil until no longer pink. Remove from the skillet. In the same skillet, saute the mushrooms in remaining oil until tender.

2. In a Dutch oven, saute garlic in butter for 1 minute. Stir in flour until blended; gradually add milk. Bring to a boil; cook and stir for 1-2 minutes or until thickened. Stir in the red peppers, mozzarella and provolone cheese, ½ cup Parmesan cheese, mushrooms and chicken.

3. Drain pasta; stir into sauce. Divide between two greased 8-in.-square baking dishes. Sprinkle each with remaining Parmesan cheese. Cover and freeze one casserole for up to 3 months. Cover and bake the remaining casserole at 350° for 30-35 minutes or until bubbly.

TO USE FROZEN CASSEROLE *Thaw in the refrigerator overnight. Remove from the refrigerator 30 minutes before baking. Cover and bake at 350° for 60-70 minutes or until bubbly, stirring once.*

Turkey & Spinach Stuffing Casserole

I know dried cranberries may seem like an odd ingredient for this dish, but they add just a little tang to make this simple casserole special.

—GILDA LESTER MILLSBORO, DE

START TO FINISH: 25 MIN.
MAKES: 4 SERVINGS

- 1 can (14½ ounces) reduced-sodium chicken broth
- 3 tablespoons butter
- 3 cups stuffing mix
- 3 cups cubed cooked turkey
- 2 cups fresh baby spinach
- ½ cup dried cranberries
- ¾ cup shredded cheddar cheese

1. Preheat oven to 350°. In a large saucepan, bring broth and butter to a boil. Remove from heat. Add stuffing mix; stir until moistened. Stir in turkey, spinach and cranberries.

2. Transfer to a greased 11x7-in. baking dish. Sprinkle with cheese. Bake, uncovered, 10-15 minutes or until cheese is melted.

Potato-Topped Chicken Casserole

A friend gave me this easy and delicious recipe. Any cheese you have on hand will work fine. The extra casserole is perfect for those nights when you want something homemade and substantial but don't have much time.

—MARY ANN DELL PHOENIXVILLE, PA

PREP: 45 MIN. • **BAKE:** 15 MIN.
MAKES: 2 CASSEROLES (6 SERVINGS EACH)

- 4 pounds medium red potatoes, quartered
- 3 pounds ground chicken
- 4 medium carrots, finely chopped
- 2 medium onions, finely chopped
- ¼ cup all-purpose flour
- 2 tablespoons tomato paste
- 1½ teaspoons salt
- ¾ teaspoon pepper
- ¼ teaspoon minced fresh thyme
- 1¼ cups chicken broth
- 1 cup milk
- 6 tablespoons butter, cubed
- 1¾ cups (7 ounces) shredded cheddar cheese

1. Place potatoes in a Dutch oven and cover with water. Bring to a boil. Reduce heat; cover and simmer for 15-20 minutes or until tender.

2. Meanwhile, in a Dutch oven, cook chicken, carrots and onions over medium heat until meat is no longer pink; drain. Stir in flour, tomato paste, salt, pepper and thyme. Add chicken broth; bring to a boil. Reduce heat; simmer, uncovered, 6-8 minutes or until thickened.

3. Preheat oven to 400°. Divide mixture between two greased 13x9-in. baking dishes. Drain potatoes; place in a large bowl. Add milk and butter; mash until smooth. Stir in cheese. Spread over chicken mixture.

4. Bake, uncovered, 15-20 minutes or until bubbly.

FREEZE OPTION *Cover and freeze unbaked casseroles up to 3 months. To use, thaw in refrigerator overnight. Remove from refrigerator 30 minutes before baking. Preheat oven to 400°. Bake, uncovered, 50-55 minutes or until bubbly.*

HOW TO

FREEZE TOMATO PASTE
❶ Line a baking sheet with waxed paper. Mound the tomato paste in 1-tablespoon portions on top of waxed paper.
❷ Freeze until firm, then transfer paste portions into a resealable freezer bag.

TURKEY & SPINACH STUFFING CASSEROLE

Chicken Lasagna

For a cooking class several years ago, I lightened up a classic lasagna with this chicken version. My class preferred it to the traditional dish in taste tests—and my family and friends did, too!

—DENA STAPELMAN LAUREL, NE

PREP: 50 MIN. • **BAKE:** 30 MIN. + STANDING
MAKES: 12 SERVINGS

- 10 uncooked lasagna noodles
- 1 pound boneless skinless chicken breasts
- 1 can (14½ ounces) diced tomatoes, undrained
- 1 can (12 ounces) tomato paste
- 1½ cups sliced fresh mushrooms
- ¼ cup chopped onion
- 1 tablespoon dried basil
- 1¾ teaspoons salt, divided
- ⅛ teaspoon garlic powder
- 3 cups (24 ounces) 2% cottage cheese
- ½ cup egg substitute
- ½ cup grated Parmesan cheese
- ⅓ cup minced fresh parsley
- ½ teaspoon pepper
- 2 cups (8 ounces) shredded part-skim mozzarella cheese

1. Cook noodles according to package directions. Meanwhile, broil chicken 6 in. from the heat until juices run clear; let stand for 15 minutes or until cool enough to handle. Shred the chicken with two forks. Drain noodles; set aside.
2. In a large nonstick skillet, combine the shredded chicken, tomatoes, tomato paste, mushrooms, onion, basil, ¾ teaspoon salt and garlic powder. Bring to a boil. Reduce heat; cover and simmer for 25-30 minutes. In a bowl, combine the cottage cheese, egg substitute, Parmesan cheese, parsley, pepper and remaining salt.
3. In a 13x9-in. baking dish coated with cooking spray, place half of the noodles, overlapping them. Layer with half of the cheese mixture, chicken mixture and mozzarella. Repeat layers. Cover and bake at 375° for 25-30 minutes or until bubbly. Uncover; bake 5 minutes longer. Let stand for 15 minutes before cutting.

TURKEY CORDON BLEU CASSEROLE

FREEZE IT

Turkey Cordon Bleu Casserole

We love everything about traditional cordon bleu, and this variation is so easy to make.

—KRISTINE BLAUERT WABASHA, MN

PREP: 20 MIN. • **BAKE:** 25 MIN.
MAKES: 8 SERVINGS

- 2 cups uncooked elbow macaroni
- 2 cans (10¾ ounces each) condensed cream of chicken soup, undiluted
- ¾ cup 2% milk
- ¼ cup grated Parmesan cheese
- 1 teaspoon prepared mustard
- 1 teaspoon paprika
- ½ teaspoon dried rosemary, crushed
- ¼ teaspoon garlic powder
- ⅛ teaspoon rubbed sage
- 2 cups cubed cooked turkey
- 2 cups cubed fully cooked ham
- 2 cups (8 ounces) shredded part-skim mozzarella cheese
- ¼ cup crushed Ritz crackers

1. Preheat oven to 350°. Cook macaroni according to package directions.
2. Meanwhile, in a large bowl, whisk soup, milk, Parmesan cheese, mustard and seasonings. Stir in turkey, ham and mozzarella cheese.
3. Drain macaroni; add to soup mixture and toss to combine. Transfer to eight greased 8-oz. ramekins. Sprinkle with crushed crackers. Bake, uncovered, 25-30 minutes or until bubbly.

FREEZE OPTION *Cover and freeze unbaked casserole. To use, partially thaw in refrigerator overnight. Remove from refrigerator 30 minutes before baking. Preheat oven to 350°. Bake as directed, increasing time as necessary to heat through and for a thermometer inserted in center to read 165°.*

Simple Creamy Chicken Enchiladas

This is one of the first recipes I created and cooked for my husband. He was so impressed! Now we fix this wonderful dish for friends regularly.

—**MELISSA ROGERS** TUSCALOOSA, AL

PREP: 30 MIN. • **BAKE:** 30 MIN.
MAKES: 2 CASSEROLES (5 SERVINGS EACH)

- 1 rotisserie chicken
- 2 cans (14½ ounces each) diced tomatoes with mild green chilies, undrained
- 2 cans (10¾ ounces each) condensed cream of chicken soup, undiluted
- 1 can (10¾ ounces) condensed cheddar cheese soup, undiluted
- ¼ cup 2% milk
- 1 tablespoon ground cumin
- 1 tablespoon chili powder
- 2 teaspoons garlic powder
- 2 teaspoons dried oregano
- 1 package (8 ounces) cream cheese, cubed
- 20 flour tortillas (8 inches), warmed
- 4 cups shredded Mexican cheese blend

1. Preheat oven to 350°. Remove meat from bones; discard bones. Shred chicken with two forks and set aside. In a large bowl, combine the tomatoes, soups, milk and seasonings. Transfer 3½ cups to another bowl; add chicken and cream cheese.

2. Spread ¼ cup soup mixture into each of two greased 13x9-in. baking dishes. Place ⅓ cup chicken mixture down the center of each tortilla. Roll up and place seam side down in baking dishes. Pour the remaining soup mixture over tops; sprinkle tops with cheese.

3. Bake, uncovered, 30-35 minutes or until heated through and cheese is melted.

FREEZE OPTION *Cover and freeze unbaked casseroles up to 3 months. To use, partially thaw in refrigerator overnight. Remove from refrigerator 30 minutes before baking. Preheat oven to 350°. Cover casserole with foil, increasing covered time to 45 minutes or until heated through and a thermometer inserted in center reads 165°. Uncover; bake 5-10 minutes longer or until cheese is melted.*

**MARY ARTHURS'
SHEPHERD'S PIE** *PAGE 57*

Pork

SAUSAGE, PEPPERONI, PORK CHOPS, HAM—YOU'LL FIND IT ALL HERE.
WITH CASSEROLES THIS HEARTY, YOU CAN'T GO WRONG.

DONETTA BRUNNER'S HAM AND ASPARAGUS CASSEROLE *PAGE 44*

NANCY MUNDHENKE'S MOSTACCIOLI *PAGE 49*

BEVERLY BATTY'S RATATOUILLE PIZZA POTPIES *PAGE 53*

Ham and Asparagus Casserole

With the freshness of asparagus and the surprise of hard-cooked eggs, this family favorite is perfect for all occasions.

—DONETTA BRUNNER SAVANNA, IL

PREP: 15 MIN. • **BAKE:** 25 MIN.
MAKES: 4 SERVINGS

- 1 package (10 ounces) frozen cut asparagus or 1 pound fresh asparagus, ½-inch cuts
- 4 hard-cooked large eggs, peeled and chopped
- 1 cup cubed fully cooked ham
- 2 tablespoons quick-cooking tapioca
- ¼ cup shredded process cheese (Velveeta)
- 2 tablespoons chopped green pepper
- 2 tablespoons chopped onion
- 1 tablespoon minced fresh parsley
- 1 tablespoon lemon juice
- ½ cup half-and-half cream or evaporated milk
- 1 cup condensed cream of mushroom soup, undiluted

TOPPING
- 1 cup soft bread crumbs
- 2 tablespoons butter, melted

1. In a large saucepan, bring ½ in. of water to a boil. Add asparagus; cover and boil for 3 minutes. Drain and immediately place asparagus in ice water. Drain and pat dry.
2. In a 2½-qt. baking dish, combine the asparagus, eggs and ham; sprinkle tapioca evenly over all. Stir in the cheese, green pepper, onion and parsley.
3. In a small bowl, combine the lemon juice, cream and soup; add to casserole and mix thoroughly. Combine topping ingredients; sprinkle over top.
4. Bake, uncovered, at 375° for 25-30 minutes or until heated through. Let stand a few minutes before serving.

PEPPERONI MACARONI

Pepperoni Macaroni

Jazz up an everyday pasta bake with pepperoni, sausage, mushrooms and olives. Because I can assemble it ahead of time and bake it right before serving, this is one of my go-to recipes when I need something on the fly.

—MARLENE MOHR CINCINNATI, OH

PREP: 15 MIN. • **BAKE:** 40 MIN.
MAKES: 8 SERVINGS

- 2½ cups uncooked elbow macaroni
- 1 pound bulk Italian sausage
- 1 large onion, chopped
- 1 can (15 ounces) pizza sauce
- 1 can (8 ounces) tomato sauce
- ⅓ cup milk
- 1 package (3½ ounces) sliced pepperoni, halved
- 1 jar (4½ ounces) sliced mushrooms, drained
- 1 can (2¼ ounces) sliced ripe olives, drained
- 1 cup (4 ounces) shredded part-skim mozzarella cheese

1. Cook macaroni according to package directions. Meanwhile, in a large skillet, cook sausage and onion over medium heat until meat is no longer pink; drain. Drain macaroni.
2. In a large bowl, combine the pizza sauce, tomato sauce and milk. Stir in the sausage mixture, macaroni, pepperoni, mushrooms and olives.
3. Transfer to a greased 13x9-in. baking dish. Cover and bake at 350° for 30 minutes. Uncover; sprinkle with cheese. Bake 10-15 minutes longer or until heated through and cheese is melted.

DID YOU KNOW?

When a *Taste of Home* recipe calls for Italian sausage, it's referring to sweet Italian sausage. Recipes using hot Italian sausage specifically call for that type of sausage.

Pork Chop and Chilies Casserole

A real estate agent who wanted to list my house dropped off this recipe at my door. I didn't end up selling the house, but the recipe has saved the day many times!

—**MICKEY O'NEAL** CHULA VISTA, CA

PREP: 15 MIN. • **BAKE:** 40 MIN.
MAKES: 4 SERVINGS

- 4 pork rib chops (¾ to 1 inch thick)
- 1 tablespoon canola oil
- 1 medium onion, chopped
- 1 can (4 ounces) chopped green chilies
- ½ cup chopped celery
- 1½ cups uncooked instant rice
- 1 can (10¾ ounces) condensed cream of mushroom soup, undiluted
- 1⅓ cups water
- 3 tablespoons reduced-sodium soy sauce

1. Preheat oven to 350°. In a large skillet, over medium-high heat, cook chops in oil over medium heat 2-3 minutes on each side or until chops are lightly browned; drain. Remove and set aside.

2. In the same skillet, saute onion, chilies and celery until onion is tender. Stir in rice; saute until lightly browned. Add remaining ingredients.

3. Place in a greased 2-qt. baking dish. Top with pork chops. Bake at 30-40 minutes or until meat is tender.

FAST FIX
Spicy Bratwurst Supper

With a zesty sauce and shredded Gouda cheese melting over the top, this hearty, delicious bratwurst dish comes together quickly in a skillet.

—*TASTE OF HOME* TEST KITCHEN

START TO FINISH: 25 MIN.
MAKES: 4 SERVINGS

- 6 bacon strips, diced
- ⅓ cup chopped onion
- 5 fully cooked bratwurst links, cut into ½-inch slices
- ½ pound sliced fresh mushrooms
- 1 tablespoon diced jalapeno pepper
- 2 cups meatless spaghetti sauce
- 2 ounces Gouda cheese, shredded
  Hot cooked rice

1. In a large skillet, cook bacon and onion over medium heat until bacon is almost crisp. Remove to paper towels to drain.

2. In the same skillet, saute the bratwurst, mushrooms and jalapeno for 3-4 minutes or until mushrooms are tender. Stir in spaghetti sauce and bacon mixture.

3. Cover and cook for 4-6 minutes or until heated through. Sprinkle with cheese. Serve with rice.

NOTE *Wear disposable gloves when cutting hot peppers; the oils can burn skin. Avoid touching your face.*

Spinach Manicotti with Ham

Everyone raves when I serve this. It's like something you'd order at an Italian restaurant, but it's so easy to make at home!

—**MICHELE NADEAU** MONROE, MI

PREP: 30 MIN. • **BAKE:** 30 MIN.
MAKES: 6 SERVINGS

- 12 uncooked manicotti shells
- ¼ cup butter, cubed
- ¼ cup all-purpose flour
- ½ teaspoon pepper
- ¼ teaspoon salt
- ¼ teaspoon ground nutmeg
- 3 cups 2% milk
- 1 carton (15 ounces) ricotta cheese
- 1 package (10 ounces) frozen chopped spinach, thawed and squeezed dry
- 2 teaspoons dried oregano
- 1½ cups cubed fully cooked ham
- ½ cup grated Parmesan cheese

1. Cook manicotti according to package directions. For sauce, in a large saucepan, melt the butter. Stir in the flour, pepper, salt and nutmeg until blended. Gradually whisk in milk. Bring to a boil. Cook and stir for 1-2 minutes or until thickened.

2. In a large bowl, combine the ricotta cheese, spinach and oregano. Stir in ham; add ½ cup sauce. Drain manicotti; stuff with ham mixture. Spread ½ cup sauce into a greased 13x9-in. baking dish. Top with stuffed manicotti. Pour remaining sauce over top; sprinkle with Parmesan cheese.

3. Cover and bake at 350° for 25-30 minutes. Uncover and bake 5 minutes longer or until golden brown.

PORK CHOP AND CHILIES CASSEROLE

SAUSAGE & SWISS CHARD LASAGNA

4. Bake, covered, 45 minutes. Bake, uncovered, 8-10 minutes longer or until cheese is melted. Let stand 10 minutes before serving.

FREEZE OPTION *Cool unbaked lasagna; cover and freeze. To use, partially thaw in refrigerator overnight. Remove from refrigerator 30 minutes before baking. Preheat oven to 350°. Cover lasagna with foil; bake as directed, increasing covered time to 55-60 minutes or until heated through and a thermometer inserted in center reads 165°. Uncover; bake 10-12 minutes longer or until bubbly.*

Parsnip & Ham au Gratin

Parsnips, thyme and a hint of roasted garlic give this entree the taste of harvesttime. The crunchy bread crumb topping makes it extra good.
—*TASTE OF HOME* TEST KITCHEN

PREP: 20 MIN. • **BAKE:** 1 HOUR
MAKES: 6 SERVINGS

- 1 **pound parsnips, peeled and sliced**
- 1 **pound Yukon Gold potatoes, peeled and sliced**
- 2 **cups cubed fully cooked ham**
- 1 **can (10¾ ounces) condensed cream of mushroom with roasted garlic soup, undiluted**
- ⅔ **cup 2% milk**
- ½ **cup grated Parmesan cheese, divided**
- ½ **teaspoon dried thyme**
- ¼ **teaspoon pepper**
- ¼ **cup dry bread crumbs**
- 2 **tablespoons butter, melted**

1. Arrange the parsnips, potatoes and ham in a greased 13x9-in. baking dish. Combine the soup, milk, ¼ cup cheese, thyme and pepper; pour over parsnip mixture.
2. In a small bowl, combine the bread crumbs, butter and remaining cheese. Sprinkle over top.
3. Cover and bake at 375° for 40 minutes. Uncover; bake 20-25 minutes longer or until potatoes are tender.

Sausage & Swiss Chard Lasagna

I discovered that this comforting, cheesy lasagna is a great way to get kids to eat healthy greens—it's such a tasty casserole they'll never suspect there's Swiss chard in there.
—**CANDACE MOREHOUSE** SHOW LOW, AZ

PREP: 45 MIN. • **BAKE:** 55 MIN. + STANDING
MAKES: 6 SERVINGS

- 1 **pound bulk Italian sausage**
- 1¾ **cups sliced fresh mushrooms**
- 2 **garlic cloves, minced**
- 1 **bunch Swiss chard (about 10 ounces)**
- 3 **tablespoons butter**
- ¼ **cup all-purpose flour**
- 3 **cups 2% milk**
- 1 **cup (4 ounces) shredded Gruyere or Swiss cheese, divided**
- 1 **tablespoon minced fresh parsley or 1 teaspoon dried parsley flakes**
- 1 **tablespoon minced fresh oregano or 1 teaspoon dried oregano**
- 1 **teaspoon grated lemon peel**
- ½ **teaspoon salt**
- ⅛ **teaspoon pepper**
- 6 **no-cook lasagna noodles**

1. Preheat oven to 350°. In a large skillet, cook sausage, mushrooms and garlic over medium heat 8-10 minutes or until sausage is no longer pink and mushrooms are tender, breaking up sausage into crumbles. Remove from pan with a slotted spoon. Remove drippings.
2. Remove stems from Swiss chard; coarsely chop leaves. In same skillet, heat butter over medium heat. Stir in flour until smooth; gradually whisk in the milk. Bring to a boil, stirring constantly; cook and stir 1-2 minutes or until thickened. Add ¾ cup cheese, parsley, oregano, lemon peel, salt and pepper; stir until cheese is melted. Stir in Swiss chard leaves.
3. Spread one-fourth of the cheese sauce into a greased 8-in.-square baking dish. Layer with each of the following: two noodles, one-third of the meat mixture and one-fourth of the cheese sauce. Repeat layers twice. Sprinkle with remaining cheese.

Zucchini Pork Chop Supper

My mom gave me a recipe for zucchini casserole, and I added the meat to make it a one-dish supper. Now I look forward to zucchini season so I can use it this way.

—LINDA MARTIN RHINEBECK, NY

PREP: 10 MIN. • **BAKE:** 1 HOUR
MAKES: 6 SERVINGS

- 1 package (14 ounces) seasoned cubed stuffing mix, divided
- ¼ cup butter, melted
- 2 pounds zucchini, cut into ½-inch pieces
- ½ cup grated carrots
- 1 can (10¾ ounces) condensed cream of celery soup, undiluted
- ½ cup milk
- 1 cup (8 ounces) sour cream
- 1 tablespoon chopped fresh parsley or 1 teaspoon dried parsley flakes
- ½ teaspoon pepper
- 6 pork loin chops (1 inch thick and 8 ounces each)
  Water or additional milk

1. In a large bowl, combine two-thirds of the stuffing mix with butter; place half in a greased 13x9-in. baking dish. In another large bowl, combine the zucchini, carrots, soup, milk, sour cream, parsley and pepper; spoon over stuffing. Sprinkle remaining buttered stuffing on top.

2. Crush remaining stuffing mix; place in a shallow bowl. In another shallow bowl, add the water or milk. Dip pork chops in water or milk, then roll in stuffing crumbs.

3. Place pork on top of stuffing mixture. Bake, uncovered, at 350° for 1 hour or until pork chops are tender.

Autumn Sausage Casserole

Apple, raisins and spices give this sausage-rice casserole a taste of autumn. We usually have it with a green salad. It would be a nice potluck dish, too—just double the recipe if needed.

—DIANE BRUNELL WASHINGTON, MA

PREP: 20 MIN. • **BAKE:** 25 MIN.
MAKES: 4-6 SERVINGS

- 1 pound bulk pork sausage
- 1 medium apple, peeled and chopped
- 1 medium onion, chopped
- ½ cup chopped celery
- 3 cups cooked long grain rice
- ½ cup raisins
- ⅓ cup minced fresh parsley
- 1 tablespoon brown sugar
- ½ teaspoon salt
- ¼ teaspoon ground allspice
- ¼ teaspoon ground cinnamon
- ⅛ teaspoon pepper

1. Preheat oven to 350°. In a large skillet, cook sausage, apple, onion and celery over medium heat until meat is no longer pink; drain. Stir in the remaining ingredients.

2. Transfer to a greased 2-qt. baking dish. Cover and bake 25-30 minutes or until heated through.

Corn Dog Casserole

Reminiscent of state fair corn dogs, this fun main dish really hits the spot.

—MARCY SUZANNE OLIPANE BELLEVILLE, IL

PREP: 25 MIN. • **BAKE:** 30 MIN.
MAKES: 12 SERVINGS

- 2 cups thinly sliced celery
- 2 tablespoons butter
- 1½ cups sliced green onions
- 1½ pounds hot dogs
- 2 large eggs
- 1½ cups 2% milk
- 2 teaspoons rubbed sage
- ¼ teaspoon pepper
- 2 packages (8½ ounces each) corn bread/muffin mix
- 2 cups (8 ounces) shredded sharp cheddar cheese, divided

1. In a small skillet, saute celery in butter 5 minutes. Add the onions; saute 5 minutes longer or until vegetables are tender. Place in a large bowl; set aside.

2. Preheat oven to 400°. Cut hot dogs lengthwise into quarters, then cut into thirds. In the same skillet, saute hot dogs 5 minutes or until lightly browned; add to vegetables. Set aside 1 cup.

3. In a large bowl, whisk eggs, milk, sage and pepper. Add remaining hot dog mixture. Stir in corn bread mixes. Add 1½ cups cheese. Spread into a shallow 3-qt. baking dish. Top with reserved hot dog mixture and remaining cheese.

4. Bake, uncovered, 30 minutes or until golden brown.

ZUCCHINI PORK CHOP SUPPER

CREAMY SPINACH
& RIGATONI BAKE

Saucy Stuffed Zucchini

Like many people I know, I've had an overabundance of zucchini in my garden. I created this recipe to use up some of my bounty. My husband often shies away from vegetable dishes, but he declared this one a winner!

—**BARBARA EDGINGTON** FRANKFORT, OH

PREP: 30 MIN. • **BAKE:** 25 MIN.
MAKES: 3-4 SERVINGS

- 3 to 4 medium zucchini (1¾ to 2 pounds)
- 12 ounces Italian sausage, cooked and drained
- ½ cup chopped sweet red pepper
- ½ cup chopped green pepper
- 2 tablespoons chopped onion
- 1½ teaspoons Italian seasoning
- 1 can (8 ounces) tomato sauce
- 2 tablespoons butter
- 2 tablespoons all-purpose flour
- ¼ teaspoon salt
- 1¼ cups milk
- ½ cup grated Parmesan cheese, divided
- 1 teaspoon Dijon mustard

1. Cut zucchini in half lengthwise. Scoop out pulp, leaving a ¼-in. shell. Reserve pulp. Cook shells in salted water for 2 minutes. Remove and drain. Set aside.

2. Chop zucchini pulp. Place pulp in a saucepan; add the sausage, peppers, onion, Italian seasoning and tomato sauce. Bring to a boil. Reduce heat; cover and simmer for 5 minutes. Place zucchini shells in a greased 13x9-in. baking dish. Spoon filling into shells.

3. In a saucepan, melt butter; whisk in flour and salt until smooth. Gradually add milk. Bring to a boil. Cook and stir for 2 minutes or until thickened and bubbly. Remove from the heat. Add ¼ cup Parmesan cheese and mustard.

4. Pour over zucchini. Sprinkle with the remaining Parmesan. Bake, uncovered, at 350° for 25-30 minutes or until heated through.

Creamy Spinach & Rigatoni Bake

Macaroni and cheese is one of the ultimate comfort foods. Why not give it a savory Italian twist?

—**TAMMY REX** NEW TRIPOLI, PA

PREP: 25 MIN. • **BAKE:** 20 MIN.
MAKES: 10 SERVINGS

- 1 package (16 ounces) rigatoni
- 8 ounces sliced pancetta, chopped
- ¾ cup butter, cubed
- ½ cup chopped onion
- ¾ cup all-purpose flour
- 1½ teaspoons salt
- ¾ teaspoon pepper
- 5¼ cups 2% milk
- 4 cups (16 ounces) shredded Italian cheese blend
- 1 can (14 ounces) water-packed artichoke hearts, rinsed, drained and chopped
- 1 package (10 ounces) frozen chopped spinach, thawed and squeezed dry
- ¼ cup shredded Parmesan cheese

1. Preheat oven to 375°. Cook rigatoni according to package directions.

2. Meanwhile, in a large skillet, cook pancetta over medium heat until crisp, stirring occasionally. Remove with a slotted spoon; drain on paper towels. Discard the drippings; wipe skillet clean.

3. In same pan, heat butter over medium-high heat. Add onion; cook and stir until tender. Stir in flour, salt and pepper until blended; gradually whisk in milk. Bring to a boil, stirring constantly; cook and stir 2-3 minutes or until thickened. Remove from heat. Stir in cheese blend until melted.

4. Stir in artichokes, spinach and pancetta. Drain rigatoni; add to cheese sauce. Transfer to a greased 13x9-in. baking dish; sprinkle with Parmesan cheese.

5. Bake, uncovered, 20-25 minutes or until golden brown and bubbly.

The Firehouse Special

This versatile dish is good for breakfast, lunch or dinner. I top each portion with salsa, sour cream or both.

—DARRELL ALVORD BOISE, ID

PREP: 45 MIN. • **BAKE:** 55 MIN.
MAKES: 2 CASSEROLES (10 SERVINGS EACH)

- 2 cans (14½ ounces each) chicken broth
- 3 cups uncooked instant rice
- 4 tablespoons butter, divided
- 2 pounds ground beef
- 2 packages (12 ounces each) bulk spicy pork sausage
- 1 pound sliced fresh mushrooms
- 3 garlic cloves, minced
- 2 packages (10 ounces each) frozen chopped spinach, thawed and squeezed dry
- 2 cups (16 ounces) 4% cottage cheese
- 8 large eggs, lightly beaten
- 1 envelope onion soup mix
- 1 envelope leek soup mix
- 2 teaspoons garlic powder
- 1 teaspoon Creole seasoning
- ¼ cup grated Parmesan cheese

1. Preheat oven to 350°. In a large saucepan, bring broth to a boil. Stir in rice; cover and remove from heat. Let stand 5 minutes. Stir in 2 tablespoons butter; set aside.

2. Meanwhile, in a large skillet, cook beef and sausage over medium heat until no longer pink; drain. Transfer to a large bowl.

3. In same skillet, saute mushrooms in remaining butter until tender. Add garlic; cook 1 minute longer. Add to meat mixture. Stir in spinach, cottage cheese, eggs, soup mixes, garlic powder, Creole seasoning and reserved rice mixture.

4. Divide between two greased 13x9-in. baking dishes; sprinkle with cheese. Cover and bake 45 minutes. Uncover; bake 10-15 minutes longer or until heated through.

NOTE *The following spices may be substituted for 1 teaspoon Creole seasoning: ¼ teaspoon each salt, garlic powder and paprika, and a pinch each of dried thyme, ground cumin and cayenne pepper.*

Mostaccioli

Even though we're not Italian, this rich pasta dish is a family tradition for holidays and other special occasions. It tastes just like a lasagna without the layering work.

—NANCY MUNDHENKE KINSLEY, KS

PREP: 15 MIN. • **BAKE:** 45 MIN.
MAKES: 10-12 SERVINGS

- 1 pound uncooked mostaccioli
- 1½ pounds bulk Italian sausage
- 1 jar (28 ounces) meatless spaghetti sauce
- 1 large egg, lightly beaten
- 1 carton (15 ounces) ricotta cheese
- 2 cups (8 ounces each) shredded part-skim mozzarella cheese
- ½ cup grated Romano cheese

1. Cook pasta according to package directions; drain. Crumble sausage into a Dutch oven. Cook over medium heat until no longer pink; drain. Stir in spaghetti sauce and pasta. In a large bowl, combine the egg, ricotta cheese and mozzarella cheese.

2. Spoon half of the pasta mixture into a greased shallow 3-qt. baking dish; layer with cheese mixture and remaining pasta mixture.

3. Cover and bake at 375° for 40 minutes or until a thermometer reads 160°. Uncover; top with Romano cheese. Bake 5 minutes longer or until heated through.

MOSTACCIOLI

Tomato, Sausage & Cheddar Bread Pudding

This savory dish is the perfect excuse to make bread pudding the main event, not merely the dessert.

—**HOLLY JONES** KENNESAW, GA

PREP: 30 MIN. • **BAKE:** 45 MIN.
MAKES: 12 SERVINGS

- 3 **cups (12 ounces) shredded sharp cheddar cheese**
- 1 **can (28 ounces) diced tomatoes, drained**
- 1 **pound bulk Italian sausage, cooked and crumbled**
- 4 **green onions, thinly sliced**
- ¼ **cup minced fresh basil or 1 tablespoon dried basil**
- ¼ **cup packed brown sugar**
- 1 **teaspoon dried oregano**
- 1 **teaspoon garlic powder**
- 3 **cups cubed French bread**
- 6 **large eggs**
- 1½ **cups heavy whipping cream**
- ½ **teaspoon salt**
- ½ **teaspoon pepper**
- ½ **cup grated Parmesan cheese**

1. Preheat oven to 350°. In a large bowl, combine the first eight ingredients. Stir in bread. Transfer to a greased 13x9-in. baking dish.

2. In the same bowl, whisk eggs, cream, salt and pepper; pour over bread mixture. Sprinkle with Parmesan cheese. Bake 45-50 minutes or until a knife inserted near the center comes out clean.

Italian Sausage Rigatoni Bake

Here's a dish that combines our favorite flavors, but it's all the gooey mozzarella that really sets it apart!

—**BLAIR LONERGAN** ROCHELLE, VA

PREP: 30 MIN. • **BAKE:** 25 MIN.
MAKES: 2 CASSEROLES (4 SERVINGS EACH)

- 1 **package (16 ounces) rigatoni**
- 1 **pound bulk Italian sausage**
- 8 **ounces sliced fresh mushrooms**
- 1 **medium sweet red pepper, chopped**
- 5 **cups marinara sauce**
- ¼ **cup grated Parmesan cheese**
- 2 **tablespoons half-and-half cream**
- 16 **ounces sliced part-skim mozzarella cheese**

1. Preheat oven to 375°. Cook rigatoni according to package directions; drain.

2. In a large skillet, cook sausage, mushrooms and pepper over medium-high heat 8-10 minutes or until sausage is no longer pink and vegetables are tender, breaking up sausage into crumbles; drain. Stir in marinara sauce, Parmesan cheese and cream. Add rigatoni and toss to coat.

3. In each of two greased 8-in.-square baking dishes, layer one-fourth of the rigatoni mixture and one-fourth of the mozzarella cheese. Repeat layers. Bake, uncovered, 25-35 minutes or until heated through and cheese is melted. (Cover loosely with foil if top browns too quickly.)

FREEZE OPTION *Cool unbaked casseroles; cover and freeze. To use, partially thaw in refrigerator overnight. Remove from refrigerator 30 minutes before baking. Preheat oven to 375°. Bake casseroles as directed, increasing time as necessary to heat through and for a thermometer inserted in center to read 165°.*

Cauliflower Ham Casserole

Cauliflower replaces the usual potatoes in this homey supper, which I've made for many years. Whenever we have leftover ham, my husband asks for this.

—**SUE HERLUND** WHITE BEAR LAKE, MN

PREP: 20 MIN. • **BAKE:** 40 MIN.
MAKES: 6 SERVINGS

- 4 **cups chopped fresh cauliflower**
- ¼ **cup butter, cubed**
- ⅓ **cup all-purpose flour**
- 2 **cups 2% milk**
- 1 **cup (4 ounces) shredded cheddar cheese**
- ½ **cup sour cream**
- 2 **cups cubed fully cooked ham**
- 1 **jar (4½ ounces) sliced mushrooms, drained**

TOPPING

- 1 **cup soft bread crumbs**
- 1 **tablespoon butter, melted**

1. Place cauliflower in a large saucepan; cover with 1 in. water. Bring to a boil. Reduce heat; cover and simmer for 5-10 minutes or until tender.

2. Meanwhile, in another large saucepan, melt butter. Stir in flour until smooth; gradually add milk. Bring to a boil; cook and stir for 2 minutes or until thickened. Remove from the heat. Stir in the cheese and sour cream until melted.

3. Drain cauliflower. In a large bowl, combine the cauliflower, ham and mushrooms. Add cheese sauce and toss to coat. Transfer to a greased 2-qt. baking dish.

4. Combine topping ingredients; sprinkle over casserole. Bake, uncovered, at 350° for 40-45 minutes or until heated through.

ITALIAN SAUSAGE RIGATONI BAKE

Italian Shepherd's Pie

For a stick-to-your-ribs main dish, give this pie a try! The Italian sausage goes so well with mashed potatoes, and both get a new twist served in a crust and cut into wedges. My family is always glad to see this casserole on the table.
—CINDY GAGE BLAIR, NE

PREP: 20 MIN. • **BAKE:** 50 MIN.
MAKES: 6-8 SERVINGS

- 1 unbaked pastry shell (9 inches)
- 1 pound bulk Italian sausage
- 1 cup (8 ounces) cream-style cottage cheese
- 1 large egg
- 1½ cups warm mashed potatoes (without added milk and butter)
- ¼ cup sour cream
- ½ teaspoon dried oregano
- ½ to ¾ teaspoon salt
- ⅛ teaspoon pepper
- 2 teaspoons butter, melted
- 1 cup (4 ounces) shredded cheddar cheese
  Cherry tomatoes, quartered
  Minced fresh parsley, optional

1. Line unpricked pastry shell with a double thickness of heavy-duty foil. Bake at 450° for 7 minutes. Remove from the oven and remove foil; set aside. Reduce heat to 350°.

2. In a large skillet, cook sausage until no longer pink; drain well on paper towels. Place cottage cheese and egg in a blender; cover and process until smooth. Transfer to a large bowl; stir in potatoes, sour cream, oregano, salt and pepper.

3. Place sausage in pastry shell; top with potato mixture. Drizzle with butter. Bake for 50-60 minutes or until a thermometer reads 160°. Sprinkle with cheese; let stand until melted. Garnish with tomatoes tossed with minced parsley if desired.

POLISH CASSEROLE

Polish Casserole

FREEZE IT

When I first made this dish, my 2-year-old liked it so much that he wanted it for every meal! If you don't have penne, you can use any pasta that will hold the sauce.
—CRYSTAL BRUNS ILIFF, CO

PREP: 25 MIN. • **BAKE:** 45 MIN.
MAKES: 2 CASSEROLES (6 SERVINGS EACH)

- 4 cups uncooked penne pasta
- 1½ pounds smoked Polish sausage or kielbasa, cut into ½-inch slices
- 2 cans (10¾ ounces each) condensed cream of mushroom soup, undiluted
- 1 jar (16 ounces) sauerkraut, rinsed and well drained
- 3 cups (12 ounces) shredded Swiss cheese, divided
- 1⅓ cups 2% milk
- 4 green onions, chopped
- 2 tablespoons Dijon mustard
- 4 garlic cloves, minced

1. Preheat oven to 350°. Cook the pasta according to package directions; drain and transfer to a large bowl. Stir in the sausage, soup, sauerkraut, 2 cups cheese, milk, onions, mustard and garlic.

2. Spoon into two greased 8-in.-square baking dishes; sprinkle with remaining cheese. Bake, uncovered, 45-50 minutes or until golden brown and bubbly.

FREEZE OPTION *Cover and freeze one casserole for up to 3 months. Thaw in the refrigerator overnight. Remove from the refrigerator 30 minutes before baking. Bake casserole, uncovered, at 350° for 50-55 minutes or until golden brown and bubbly.*

Ham and Broccoli Biscuit Bake

Whenever I cook this creamy dish, I'm on alert to make sure my husband doesn't nibble before I can bring it to the table. I chide him, but really, who could resist the aroma or the bubbling crust?

—**AMY WHEELER** BALTIMORE, MD

PREP: 20 MIN. • **BAKE:** 25 MIN.
MAKES: 6 SERVINGS

- 2½ cups frozen chopped broccoli
- 1 can (10¾ ounces) condensed cream of potato soup, undiluted
- 1¼ cups 2% milk, divided
- 1 teaspoon garlic pepper blend
- ½ teaspoon crushed red pepper flakes
- ¼ teaspoon pepper
- 2 cups cubed fully cooked ham
- 1 cup (4 ounces) shredded cheddar-Monterey Jack cheese
- 1½ cups biscuit/baking mix
- 1 large egg

1. Preheat oven to 350°. Combine broccoli, soup, ¾ cup milk and seasonings in a large saucepan; bring to a boil. Reduce heat; stir in ham and cheese. Cook and stir until cheese is melted. Pour into a greased 11x7-in. baking dish.
2. Combine biscuit mix, egg and remaining milk in a small bowl just until moistened. Drop by tablespoonfuls over ham mixture; spread gently.
3. Bake, uncovered, 25-30 minutes or until golden brown.

Ratatouille Pizza Potpies

A homemade bread crust covers a bubbly Italian-style stew featuring pizza sauce, vegetables and cheese. The individual pies are really hearty!

—**BEVERLY BATTY** FOREST LAKE, MN

PREP: 45 MIN. + RISING • **BAKE:** 20 MIN.
MAKES: 8 SERVINGS

- 1½ teaspoons active dry yeast
- 1 cup warm water (110° to 115°)
- 1 tablespoon olive oil
- 1 tablespoon honey
- 1½ teaspoons salt
- 2½ to 3 cups bread flour

FILLING
- 1 jar (14 ounces) pizza sauce
- 1 small eggplant, peeled and cut into ½-inch cubes
- 1 small zucchini, cut into ½-inch cubes
- 1 medium sweet red pepper, chopped
- 1 medium sweet yellow pepper, chopped
- 1 small onion, chopped
- 4 ounces sliced pepperoni
- 1 cup (4 ounces) shredded part-skim mozzarella cheese
- ¾ cup shredded provolone cheese
- ¾ cup shredded Asiago cheese
- ¾ cup grated Parmesan cheese
- 2 teaspoons honey
- 1 garlic clove, minced
- 1 teaspoon garlic salt
- 1 teaspoon pizza or Italian seasoning
- 1 teaspoon dried oregano
- 1 tablespoon olive oil

1. In a large bowl, dissolve yeast in warm water. Add the oil, honey, salt and 1½ cups flour. Beat until smooth. Stir in enough remaining flour to form a soft dough (dough will be sticky).
2. Turn onto a floured surface; knead until smooth and elastic, about 6-8 minutes. Place in a greased bowl, turning once to grease the top. Cover and let rise in a warm place until doubled, about 1 hour.
3. In a large bowl, combine the pizza sauce, vegetables, pepperoni, cheeses, honey, garlic and seasonings; divide among eight 10-oz. ramekins or custard cups.
4. Punch dough down. Divide dough into eight portions. On a lightly floured surface, roll out dough to fit ramekins. Cut out a decorative center with a small Christmas cookie cutter or small cookie cutter of your choice. Place dough over filling; trim and seal edges. Brush with oil.
5. Place ramekins on a baking sheet. Bake at 375° for 20-25 minutes or until filling is bubbly and crust is golden brown.
NOTE *To make this recipe in one dish; transfer filling to a greased 11x7-in. baking dish. Top with prepared dough and brush with oil. Bake at 375° for 30-35 minutes or until filling is bubbly and crust is golden brown.*

HAM AND BROCCOLI BISCUIT BAKE

SAUSAGE LASAGNA ROLLS

PORK

Chili Cheese Dog Casserole

If you like corn bread with your chili, you've got to try this main dish. The kids will especially love the cheesy hot dog bites—and you'll like them, too!
—*TASTE OF HOME* TEST KITCHEN

PREP: 20 MIN. • **BAKE:** 30 MIN.
MAKES: 6 SERVINGS

- 1 **package (8½ ounces) corn bread/muffin mix**
- 1 **cup chopped green pepper**
- ½ **cup chopped onion**
- ½ **cup chopped celery**
- 1 **tablespoon olive oil**
- 1 **package (1 pound) hot dogs, halved lengthwise and cut into bite-size pieces**
- 1 **can (15 ounces) chili with beans**
- 2 **tablespoons brown sugar**
- ½ **teaspoon garlic powder**
- ½ **teaspoon chili powder**
- 1 **cup (4 ounces) shredded cheddar cheese, divided**

1. Prepare corn bread batter according to package directions. Spread half the batter into a greased 8-in.-square baking dish; set aside.
2. In a large skillet, saute the green pepper, onion and celery in oil until crisp-tender. Stir in hot dogs; saute 3-4 minutes longer or until lightly browned. Stir in the chili, brown sugar, garlic powder and chili powder; heat through. Stir in ¾ cup cheese.
3. Spoon over corn bread batter; top with remaining corn bread batter. Sprinkle the remaining cheese over the top.
4. Bake, uncovered, at 350° for 28-32 minutes or until a toothpick inserted near the center comes out clean. Let stand for 5 minutes before serving.

FREEZE IT

Sausage Lasagna Rolls

Who said lasagna noodles have to lie flat? This artful interpretation of layered comfort food—with a twist—is what I like to call "casse-roll."
—**KALI WRASPIR** OLYMPIA, WA

PREP: 45 MIN. • **BAKE:** 45 MIN.
MAKES: 2 CASSEROLES (6 SERVINGS EACH)

- 12 **lasagna noodles**
- 1 **pound bulk Italian sausage**
- 2 **jars (26 ounces each) spaghetti sauce**
- 1 **carton (15 ounces) ricotta cheese**
- 2 **cups (8 ounces) shredded part-skim mozzarella cheese, divided**
- ¾ **cup shredded Parmesan cheese, divided**
- 1 **large egg**
- 2 **tablespoons minced fresh parsley or 2 teaspoons dried parsley flakes**
- 2½ **teaspoons minced fresh rosemary or ¾ teaspoon dried rosemary, crushed**
- 2 **teaspoons lemon juice**
- 1½ **teaspoons minced fresh thyme or ½ teaspoon dried thyme**
- 1 **teaspoon grated lemon peel**
- 1 **teaspoon coarsely ground pepper**
- ½ **teaspoon salt**

1. Preheat oven to 350°. Cook noodles according to package directions.
2. Meanwhile, in a large skillet, cook the sausage over medium heat until no longer pink; drain. Stir in the spaghetti sauce.
3. In a large bowl, combine ricotta, 1 cup mozzarella, ¼ cup Parmesan, egg, parsley, rosemary, lemon juice, thyme, lemon peel, pepper and salt. Drain noodles. Spread 2 tablespoons cheese mixture on each noodle; carefully roll up.
4. Spread ⅔ cup meat sauce into each of two greased 11x7-in. baking dishes. Place roll-ups seam side down over sauce. Top with remaining meat sauce. Sprinkle with remaining mozzarella and Parmesan cheeses.
5. Cover and bake 45-50 minutes or until bubbly.
FREEZE OPTION *Cover and freeze unbaked casseroles up to 3 months. To use, thaw in the refrigerator overnight. Remove from refrigerator 30 minutes before baking. Preheat oven to 350°. Cover and bake 50-60 minutes or until bubbly.*

Pineapple Ham Casserole

Living in Hawaii, I wanted to share a recipe that features pineapple. It's our most important fruit crop, and it's really outstanding in this dish.

—MARSHA FLEMING KULA, HI

PREP: 15 MIN. • **BAKE:** 30 MIN.
MAKES: 4 SERVINGS

- 2 cups uncooked wide egg noodles
- ½ cup chopped celery
- 2 tablespoons butter, divided
- 1 package (8 ounces) cream cheese, cubed
- ¾ cup milk
- 2 cups cubed fully cooked ham
- 2 cans (8 ounces each) crushed pineapple, drained
- 2 teaspoons Worcestershire sauce
- ½ teaspoon salt
  Dash pepper
- ¼ cup dry bread crumbs

1. Cook noodles according to package directions; drain. In a large skillet, saute celery in 1 tablespoon butter until tender. Stir in cream cheese and milk; cook and stir until cheese is melted. Add noodles, ham, pineapple, Worcestershire sauce, salt and pepper.

2. Transfer to an ungreased 1½-qt. baking dish. Melt remaining butter; toss with bread crumbs. Sprinkle over the top. Bake, uncovered, at 350° for 30-35 minutes or until heated through.

TOP TIP

Neufchatel cheese is a soft, unripened cheese that originates in France. American Neufchatel is slightly lower in calories than cream cheese and has slightly more moisture. You can substitute Neufchatel for regular cream cheese in most recipes, but you may notice a slightly different texture in dishes that require cooking.

PINEAPPLE HAM CASSEROLE

CARNITAS WITH ORZO AND PEPPERS IN RED MOLE SAUCE

Hearty Barley Bake

Barley is a nice change of pace from the usual pasta or rice. This dish is full of spicy sausage and lots of vegetables, including spinach, carrots and corn.

—JENNY BROWNING CYPRESS, TX

PREP: 20 MIN. • **BAKE:** 45 MIN.
MAKES: 6 SERVINGS

- 2 cups sliced fresh mushrooms
- 1 cup thinly sliced carrots
- ½ cup chopped onion
- 2 teaspoons canola oil
- 1 garlic clove, minced
- 12 ounces bulk pork sausage
- 1½ cups cooked barley
- 1 can (14¾ ounces) cream-style corn
- 1 package (10 ounces) frozen chopped spinach, thawed and squeezed dry
- 3 green onions, sliced
- 1 teaspoon dried savory
- 1 teaspoon dried thyme
- ½ teaspoon dried marjoram
- ⅛ teaspoon pepper
- ½ cup shredded Parmesan cheese

1. In a large skillet, saute mushrooms, carrots and onion in oil until tender. Add garlic; cook 1 minute longer. Transfer to a large bowl.

2. In the same skillet, cook sausage over medium heat until no longer pink; drain. Add to mushroom mixture. Stir in the barley, corn, spinach, onions, savory, thyme, marjoram and pepper.

3. Transfer to a greased shallow 2-qt. baking dish. Cover and bake at 350° for 40-45 minutes or until heated through. Sprinkle with cheese. Bake, uncovered, 5 minutes longer or until the cheese is melted.

HOW TO

DRAIN SPINACH

If the spinach is cooked, allow to cool. With clean hands, squeeze the water out of the greens.

FREEZE IT

Carnitas with Orzo and Peppers in Red Mole Sauce

For a tasty way to stretch my grocery dollars, I combine pork shoulder roast with orzo, peppers and mole sauce to make this spicy Mexican comfort food.

—KARI WHEATON SOUTH BELOIT, IL

PREP: 1 HOUR 35 MIN. • **BAKE:** 40 MIN.
MAKES: 5 SERVINGS

- 1 boneless pork shoulder butt roast (1½ to 2 pounds), cut into ½-inch cubes
- 1½ teaspoons salt, divided
- ½ teaspoon pepper
- 1 cup uncooked orzo pasta
- 1 each medium green, sweet red and yellow peppers, chopped
- 2 jalapeno peppers, seeded and chopped
- 1 medium onion, chopped
- 1 tablespoon olive oil
- 1 cup chicken broth
- ¼ cup red mole sauce
- 2 tablespoons tomato paste
- 1 cup (4 ounces) quesadilla or Monterey Jack cheese, shredded

1. Place pork in a 15x10x1-in. baking pan, sprinkle with 1 teaspoon salt and ½ teaspoon pepper. Bake at 325° for 1½ hours or until tender.

2. Meanwhile, cook pasta according to package directions; drain and set aside. In a large skillet, saute peppers and onion in oil until crisp-tender. In a greased 13x9-in. baking pan, combine the orzo, peppers and onion.

3. In a small saucepan, whisk the chicken broth, mole sauce, tomato paste and remaining salt. Cook and stir until thickened and bubbly. Pour over orzo and vegetables. Stir in pork; sprinkle with cheese. Cool. Cover; may be frozen for up to 3 months.

TO USE FROZEN CARNITAS *Thaw in refrigerator overnight. Remove from the refrigerator 30 minutes before baking. Cover and bake at 350° for 35-40 minutes or until heated through. Uncover; broil 3-4 in. from the heat for 4-5 minutes or until the cheese is lightly golden.*

NOTE *To use immediately, broil as directed. When cutting hot peppers, disposable gloves are recommended.*

Ham & Tater Bake

This casserole reminds me of a loaded baked potato. I usually make it several times a month—I've even served it to company. People always ask for the recipe, which I got from my sister.

—**PEGGY GRIEME** PINEHURST, NC

PREP: 10 MIN. • **BAKE:** 40 MIN.
MAKES: 6-8 SERVINGS

- 1 package (28 ounces) frozen steak fries
- 3 cups frozen chopped broccoli, thawed and drained
- 1½ cups diced fully cooked ham
- 1 can (10¾ ounces) condensed cream of broccoli soup, undiluted
- ¾ cup milk
- ½ cup mayonnaise
- 1 cup (4 ounces) shredded cheddar cheese

1. Preheat oven to 350°. Arrange fries in a greased 3-qt. baking dish; layer with broccoli and then ham. Combine soup, milk and mayonnaise until smooth; pour over ham.
2. Cover and bake 20 minutes. Sprinkle with the cheese; bake, uncovered, 20-25 minutes longer or until bubbly.

Shepherd's Pie

Of all the shepherd's pie recipes I've tried through the years, this one is definitely the best. I enjoy cooking for friends and family, who all love this meat pie.

—**MARY ARTHURS** ETOBICOKE, ON

PREP: 30 MIN. • **BAKE:** 45 MIN.
MAKES: 6 SERVINGS

PORK LAYER
- 1 pound ground pork
- 1 small onion, chopped
- 2 garlic cloves, minced
- 1 cup cooked rice
- ½ cup pork gravy or ¼ cup chicken broth
- ½ teaspoon salt
- ½ teaspoon dried thyme

CABBAGE LAYER
- 1 medium carrot, diced
- 1 small onion, chopped
- 2 tablespoons butter or margarine
- 6 cups chopped cabbage
- 1 cup chicken broth
- ½ teaspoon salt
- ¼ teaspoon pepper

POTATO LAYER
- 2 cups mashed potatoes
- ¼ cup shredded cheddar cheese

In a skillet over medium heat, brown pork until no longer pink. Add onion and garlic. Cook until vegetables are tender; drain. Stir in rice, gravy, salt and thyme. Spoon into a greased 11x7-in. baking dish. In the same skillet, saute carrot and onion in butter over medium heat for 5 minutes. Stir in cabbage; cook for 1 minute. Add broth, salt and pepper; cover and cook for 10 minutes. Spoon over pork layer. Spoon or pipe mashed potatoes on top; sprinkle with cheese. Bake, uncovered, at 350° for 45 minutes or until browned.

SHEPHERD'S PIE

**EDIE DESPAIN'S CREAMY
TUNA-NOODLE CASSEROLE** *PAGE 63*

Fish & Seafood

AHOY! IT'S TIME TO SET SAIL ON A NEW FLAVOR VOYAGE.
THESE SURPRISING DISHES WILL REEL IN THE COMPLIMENTS.

SUNDRA HAUCK'S SUNDAY SHRIMP PASTA BAKE *PAGE 60*

ELENA HANSEN'S SEAFOOD LASAGNA *PAGE 68*

JEFFREY MACCORD'S SEAFOOD IN TOMATO SAUCE *PAGE 65*

Sunday Shrimp Pasta Bake

Pasta is popular in our home, so my ideal meal would have it in the main course. In this sensational dish, pasta complements the shrimp our local fishermen bring in.

—SUNDRA HAUCK BOGALUSA, LA

PREP: 30 MIN. • **BAKE:** 25 MIN.
MAKES: 8 SERVINGS

- 12 ounces uncooked vermicelli
- 1 medium green pepper, chopped
- 5 green onions, chopped
- 6 tablespoons butter, cubed
- 6 garlic cloves, minced
- 2 tablespoons all-purpose flour
- 2 pounds cooked medium shrimp, peeled and deveined
- 1 teaspoon celery salt
- ⅛ teaspoon pepper
- 1 pound process cheese (Velveeta), cubed
- 1 can (10 ounces) diced tomatoes and green chilies, drained
- 1 can (4 ounces) mushroom stems and pieces, drained
- 1 tablespoon grated Parmesan cheese

1. Preheat oven to 350°. Cook vermicelli according to package directions.
2. Meanwhile, in a large skillet, saute green pepper and onions in butter until tender. Add garlic; cook 1 minute longer. Gradually stir in flour until blended. Stir in shrimp, celery salt and pepper; cook, uncovered, over medium heat 5-6 minutes or until heated through.
3. In a microwave-safe bowl, combine process cheese, tomatoes and mushrooms. Microwave, uncovered, on high 3-4 minutes or until cheese is melted, stirring occasionally. Add to shrimp mixture. Drain vermicelli; stir into skillet. Pour into a greased 13x9-in. baking dish. Sprinkle with Parmesan cheese.
4. Bake, uncovered, 25-30 minutes or until heated through.

Captain Russell's Jambalaya

A tour guide in New Orleans gave me this recipe. It's a breeze to prepare! The deliciously authentic Cajun flavors make it one of my favorites.

—DONNA LAMANO OLATHE, KS

PREP: 15 MIN. • **BAKE:** 40 MIN.
MAKES: 6 SERVINGS

- 1 can (10½ ounces) condensed French onion soup
- 1¼ cups reduced-sodium beef broth
- 1 can (8 ounces) tomato sauce
- ½ cup butter, cubed
- 1 small green pepper, chopped
- 1 small onion, chopped
- 1½ teaspoons Creole seasoning
- 1 teaspoon hot pepper sauce
- 1 pound uncooked medium shrimp, peeled and deveined
- ½ pound fully cooked andouille sausage links, halved lengthwise and cut into ½-inch slices
- 2 cups uncooked long grain rice

1. Preheat oven to 375°. In a large saucepan, combine first eight ingredients. Bring to a boil. Remove from heat; stir in shrimp, sausage and rice. Transfer to a greased 13x9-in. baking dish.
2. Cover and bake 30 minutes. Remove foil and stir; cover and bake 10-15 minutes longer or until rice is tender.

NOTE *The following spices may be substituted for 1 teaspoon Creole seasoning: ¼ teaspoon each salt, garlic powder and paprika; and a pinch each of dried thyme, ground cumin and cayenne pepper.*

DID YOU KNOW?

Andouille sausage is a smoked variety made of pork seasoned with garlic. It's often used in Cajun recipes, such as jambalaya or gumbo.

CAPTAIN RUSSELL'S JAMBALAYA

SEAFOOD
AU GRATIN

Seafood au Gratin

A seafood casserole is a must for any bountiful buffet. My father was a fisherman, so we ate fish almost every day growing up. Over the years I've tasted many seafood dishes, but I don't think any were better than this one.

—**HAZEL MCMULLIN** AMHERST, NS

PREP: 30 MIN. • **BAKE:** 15 MIN.
MAKES: 6 SERVINGS

- 4 **tablespoons butter, divided**
- 2 **tablespoons all-purpose flour**
- ⅛ **teaspoon pepper**
- 1 **cup chicken broth**
- ½ **cup 2% milk**
- ½ **cup grated Parmesan cheese, divided**
- ½ **pound sea scallops**
- 1 **pound haddock or cod fillets, cut into six pieces**
- 1½ **cups sliced fresh mushrooms**
- ½ **cup shredded part-skim mozzarella cheese**
- ½ **cup shredded cheddar cheese**

1. In a large saucepan, melt 2 tablespoons butter. Stir in flour and pepper until smooth; gradually add broth and milk. Bring to a boil; cook and stir 2 minutes or until thickened. Stir in ¼ cup Parmesan cheese; set aside.
2. Preheat oven to 350°. Place scallops in another saucepan; cover with water. Simmer, uncovered, 4-5 minutes or until firm and opaque.
3. Meanwhile, place fillets in a shallow 2-qt. microwave-safe dish.

Cover and microwave on high 2-4 minutes or until fish flakes easily with a fork. Drain scallops. Arrange fish and scallops in a greased 11x7-in. baking dish.
4. In a small skillet, saute mushrooms in remaining butter until tender; stir into cheese sauce. Spoon over seafood. Sprinkle with mozzarella, cheddar and remaining Parmesan cheese.
5. Cover and bake 15-20 minutes or until bubbly and cheese is melted.

Crab Imperial Casserole

The recipe serves eight, but plan to double it if you're having folks over. Fresh mushrooms and succulent crab make it hard to turn down second helpings.

—**BARBARA CARLUCCI** ORANGE PARK, FL

PREP: 20 MIN. • **BAKE:** 25 MIN.
MAKES: 8 SERVINGS

- 3 **cups uncooked spiral pasta**
- 1¾ **cups sliced fresh mushrooms**
- 5 **tablespoons butter, cubed**
- 2 **tablespoons all-purpose flour**
- ¾ **teaspoon pepper**
- ½ **teaspoon salt**
- 1½ **cups 2% milk**
- 4 **cans (6 ounces each) lump crabmeat, drained**
- 1 **can (10¾ ounces) condensed cream of mushroom soup, undiluted**
- ¼ **cup crushed butter-flavored crackers**

1. Preheat oven to 350°. Cook pasta according to package directions.

2. Meanwhile, in a large skillet, saute mushrooms in butter until tender. Stir in flour, pepper and salt until blended; gradually add milk. Bring to a boil. Cook and stir 2 minutes or until thickened. Stir in crab and soup until blended.
3. Drain pasta. Add crab mixture; toss to coat. Transfer to a greased 13x9-in. baking dish; sprinkle with cracker crumbs.
4. Bake, uncovered, 25-30 minutes or until bubbly.

Onions Neptune

You can serve this bake as an entree or appetizer, depending on the occasion. I often add whatever ingredients I have handy, such as mushrooms or sun-dried tomatoes. Whether I serve it as is or jazz it up a bit, it's always delicious.

—**TODD NOON** GALLOWAY, NJ

PREP: 20 MIN. • **BAKE:** 35 MIN.
MAKES: 12 SERVINGS

- 5 **to 6 medium sweet onions, sliced and separated into rings**
- ½ **cup butter, softened, divided**
- 2 **cans (6 ounces each) lump crabmeat, drained, divided**
- 3 **cups (12 ounces) shredded Swiss cheese**
- 1 **can (10¾ ounces) condensed cream of mushroom soup, undiluted**
- ½ **cup evaporated milk**
- ½ **teaspoon salt**
- ¼ **teaspoon pepper**
- 12 **to 16 slices French bread (¼ inch thick)**

1. Preheat oven to at 350°. In a large skillet, saute onions in ¼ cup butter until tender. Remove from the heat; gently stir in half of the crab. Spread into a greased 13x9-in. baking dish. Top with remaining crab. Combine the cheese, soup, milk, salt and pepper; spoon over crab.
2. Spread remaining butter over one side of each slice of bread; place buttered side up over casserole. Bake, uncovered, for 35-45 minutes or until golden brown.

MINI SCALLOP CASSEROLES

Mini Scallop Casseroles

Tiny, tender bay scallops take center stage in these individual dishes. The casseroles are reminiscent of potpies— very creamy and packed with tasty veggies in every bite.
—**VIVIAN MANARY** NEPEAN, ON

PREP: 30 MIN. • **BAKE:** 20 MIN.
MAKES: 4 SERVINGS

- 3 celery ribs, chopped
- 1 cup sliced fresh mushrooms
- 1 medium green pepper, chopped
- 1 small onion, chopped
- 2 tablespoons butter
- ⅓ cup all-purpose flour
- ¼ teaspoon salt
- ¼ teaspoon pepper
- 2 cups fat-free milk
- 1 pound bay scallops

TOPPING
- 1 cup soft bread crumbs
- 1 tablespoon butter, melted
- ¼ cup shredded cheddar cheese

1. In a large skillet, saute celery, mushrooms, green pepper and onion in butter until tender. Stir in flour, salt and pepper until blended; gradually add milk. Bring to a boil; cook and stir 2 minutes or until thickened.
2. Reduce heat; add scallops. Cook, stirring occasionally, 3-4 minutes or until scallops are firm and opaque.
3. Preheat oven to 350°. Divide mixture among four 10-oz. ramekins or custard cups. In a small bowl, combine crumbs and butter; sprinkle over scallop mixture.
4. Bake, uncovered, 15-20 minutes or until bubbly. Sprinkle with cheese; bake 5 minutes longer or until cheese is melted.

TOP TIP

To keep celery fresh longer, I remove celery from the store bag and wrap it in paper towel, then in aluminum foil. Store in the refrigerator. When you need some, break off what your recipe calls for, re-wrap the rest and return to fridge. I find celery stored like this stays crisp a very long time.
—**LINDA J.** MILNER, GA

Blend of the Bayou

My sister-in-law shared this recipe with me when I first moved to Louisiana. It's been handed down in my husband's family for generations, and I've passed it on to my children, too.

—RUBY WILLIAMS BOGALUSA, LA

PREP: 20 MIN. • **BAKE:** 25 MIN.
MAKES: 6-8 SERVINGS

- 1 package (8 ounces) cream cheese, cubed
- 4 tablespoons butter, divided
- 1 large onion, chopped
- 2 celery ribs, chopped
- 1 large green pepper, chopped
- 1 pound cooked medium shrimp, peeled and deveined
- 2 cans (6 ounces each) crabmeat, drained, flaked and cartilage removed
- 1 can (10¾ ounces) condensed cream of mushroom soup, undiluted
- ¾ cup cooked rice
- 1 jar (4½ ounces) sliced mushrooms, drained
- 1 teaspoon garlic salt
- ¾ teaspoon hot pepper sauce
- ½ teaspoon cayenne pepper
- ¾ cup shredded cheddar cheese
- ½ cup crushed butter-flavored crackers (about 12 crackers)

1. Preheat oven to 350°. In a small saucepan, cook and stir cream cheese and 2 tablespoons butter over low heat until melted and smooth.

2. In a large skillet, saute onion, celery and green pepper in remaining butter until tender. Stir in shrimp, crab, soup, rice, mushrooms, garlic salt, pepper sauce, cayenne and cream cheese mixture.

3. Transfer to a greased 2-qt. baking dish. Combine cheddar cheese and cracker crumbs; sprinkle over top. Bake, uncovered, 25-30 minutes or until bubbly.

Creamy Tuna-Noodle Casserole

When you need supper fast, this tuna casserole with peas, peppers and onions makes a super meal in one dish. Cooked chicken breast will also work nicely in place of the tuna.

—EDIE DESPAIN LOGAN, UT

PREP: 20 MIN. • **BAKE:** 25 MIN.
MAKES: 6 SERVINGS

- 5 cups uncooked egg noodles
- 1 cup frozen peas
- 1 can (10¾ ounces) reduced-fat reduced-sodium condensed cream of mushroom soup, undiluted
- 1 cup (8 ounces) fat-free sour cream
- ⅔ cup grated Parmesan cheese
- ⅓ cup 2% milk
- ¼ teaspoon salt
- 2 cans (5 ounces each) light tuna in water, drained and flaked
- ¼ cup finely chopped onion
- ¼ cup finely chopped green pepper

TOPPING
- ½ cup soft bread crumbs
- 1 tablespoon butter, melted

1. Preheat oven to 350°. Cook noodles according to package directions for al dente, adding peas during the last minute of cooking; drain.

2. Meanwhile, in a large bowl, combine soup, sour cream, cheese, milk and salt; stir in tuna, onion and pepper. Add noodles and peas; toss to combine.

3. Transfer to an 11x7-in. baking dish coated with cooking spray. In a small bowl, toss bread crumbs with melted butter; sprinkle over top. Bake, uncovered, 25-30 minutes or until bubbly.

NOTE *To make soft bread crumbs, tear bread into pieces and place in a food processor or blender. Cover and pulse until crumbs form. One slice of bread makes ½ to ¾ cup crumbs.*

CREAMY TUNA-NOODLE CASSEROLE

CRAB 'N' PENNE CASSEROLE

Crab 'n' Penne Casserole

A jar of Alfredo sauce lends creaminess to this crab casserole, while red pepper flakes kick up the taste. To round the dish out, summer squash and zucchini bring garden-fresh goodness.

—**BERNADETTE BENNETT** WACO, TX

PREP: 20 MIN. • **BAKE:** 40 MIN.
MAKES: 6 SERVINGS

- 1½ cups uncooked penne pasta
- 1 jar (15 ounces) Alfredo sauce
- 1½ cups imitation crabmeat, chopped
- 1 medium yellow summer squash, sliced
- 1 medium zucchini, sliced
- 1 tablespoon dried parsley flakes
- ⅛ to ¼ teaspoon crushed red pepper flakes
- 1½ cups (6 ounces) shredded part-skim mozzarella cheese
- 2 tablespoons dry bread crumbs
- 2 teaspoons butter, melted

1. Preheat oven to 325°. Cook pasta according to package directions.
2. Meanwhile, in a large bowl, combine Alfredo sauce, crab, yellow squash, zucchini, parsley and pepper flakes. Drain pasta; add to sauce mixture and toss to coat. Transfer to a greased 13x9-in. baking dish. Sprinkle with cheese.

3. Cover and bake 35 minutes or until heated through. Toss bread crumbs and butter; sprinkle over casserole. Bake, uncovered, 5-6 minutes longer or until browned.
CRAB AND TWIST BAKE *Substitute spiral pasta for the penne and provolone cheese for the mozzarella.*

Southwest Tuna-Noodle Casserole

Surprisingly, none of my co-workers had ever tried tuna-noodle casserole. Since we live near the Mexican border, they challenged me to make a Southwest version. After trying the tasty results, everyone wanted the recipe!

—**SANDRA CRANE** LAS CRUCES, NM

PREP: 20 MIN. • **BAKE:** 30 MIN.
MAKES: 6 SERVINGS

- 1 package (16 ounces) egg noodles
- 2½ cups milk
- 1 can (12 ounces) light tuna in water, drained
- 1 can (10¾ ounces) condensed cream of chicken soup, undiluted
- 1 can (10¾ ounces) condensed cream of mushroom soup, undiluted
- 1 cup (4 ounces) shredded cheddar cheese
- 1 can (4 ounces) chopped green chilies
- 2 cups crushed tortilla chips

1. Cook noodles according to package directions. Meanwhile, in a large bowl, combine the milk, tuna, soups, cheese and chilies. Drain noodles; gently stir into tuna mixture.
2. Transfer to an ungreased 13x9-in. baking dish. Sprinkle with tortilla chips. Bake, uncovered, at 350° for 30-35 minutes or until bubbly.

Cheesy Clam Manicotti

I created this recipe when I was having company and couldn't decide whether to serve seafood or Italian. It was a big hit! I usually add a little extra hot sauce.

—**KATHY KYSAR** HOMER, AK

PREP: 30 MIN. • **BAKE:** 25 MIN.
MAKES: 4 SERVINGS

- 1 jar (24 ounces) meatless spaghetti sauce
- ¼ teaspoon hot pepper sauce
- 2 cans (6½ ounces each) minced clams
- 1 carton (8 ounces) ricotta cheese
- 4 ounces cream cheese, softened
- ¼ cup spreadable chive and onion cream cheese
- 2 cups (8 ounces) shredded part-skim mozzarella cheese
- ⅓ cup grated Parmesan cheese
- 1 teaspoon minced garlic
- ½ teaspoon pepper
- ¼ teaspoon dried oregano
- 8 manicotti shells, cooked and drained

1. In a large saucepan, combine spaghetti sauce and hot pepper sauce. Drain one can of clams; add clams to sauce. Stir in clams and juice from second can. Bring to a boil. Reduce heat; simmer, uncovered, for 20 minutes.
2. Meanwhile, in a large bowl, beat ricotta and cream cheeses until smooth. Stir in the cheeses, garlic, pepper and oregano. Stuff into manicotti shells.
3. Preheat the oven to 350°. Spread ¾ cup clam sauce into a greased 11x7-in. baking dish. Arrange manicotti over sauce; top with remaining sauce.
4. Bake, uncovered, for 25-30 minutes or until bubbly. Let stand for 5 minutes before serving.

Shrimp and Fontina Casserole

Looking for a gourmet seafood recipe? Try this one. The Cajun flavor comes through the cheese topping, and the confetti of green onions and red peppers makes it pretty enough for guests.

—EMORY DOTY JASPER, GA

PREP: 35 MIN. • **BAKE:** 15 MIN. + STANDING
MAKES: 8 SERVINGS

- ½ cup all-purpose flour
- 1 tablespoon Cajun seasoning
- ½ teaspoon pepper
- 2 pounds uncooked large shrimp, peeled and deveined
- 2 tablespoons olive oil
- 4 thin slices prosciutto or deli ham, cut into thin strips
- ½ pound medium fresh mushrooms, quartered
- 2 tablespoons butter
- 4 green onions, chopped
- 2 garlic cloves, minced
- 1 cup heavy whipping cream
- 8 ounces fontina cheese, cubed
- 1 jar (7 ounces) roasted sweet red peppers, drained and chopped
- ¼ cup grated Parmigiano-Reggiano cheese
- ¼ cup grated Romano cheese

1. Preheat oven to 350°. In a large resealable plastic bag, combine the flour, Cajun seasoning and pepper. Add shrimp, a few at a time, and shake to coat.

2. In a large skillet over medium heat, cook shrimp in oil in batches until golden brown. Drain on paper towels. Transfer to an ungreased 13x9-in. baking dish; top with prosciutto strips. Set aside.

3. In the same skillet, saute mushrooms in butter until tender. Add onions and garlic; cook 1 minute longer. Add cream and fontina cheese; cook and stir until cheese is melted. Remove from heat; stir in peppers. Pour over prosciutto. Sprinkle with remaining cheeses.

4. Bake, uncovered, 15-20 minutes or until bubbly and cheese is melted. Let stand 10 minutes before serving.

Seafood in Tomato Sauce

We live near the Chesapeake Bay and reap its bountiful seafood harvest. I serve this to company often, to rave reviews. I hope you'll enjoy it as much as my family does!

—JEFFREY MACCORD NEW CASTLE, DE

PREP: 20 MIN. • **COOK:** 45 MIN.
MAKES: 4 SERVINGS

- 1¾ cups sliced fresh mushrooms
- 1 garlic clove, minced
- 3 tablespoons canola oil, divided
- 1 can (14½ ounces) diced tomatoes, drained
- 1½ teaspoons dried oregano
- 1 teaspoon sugar
- 1 teaspoon dried thyme
  Salt and pepper to taste
- ½ pound lump crabmeat or imitation crabmeat
- ½ pound bay scallops
- ½ pound uncooked small shrimp, peeled and deveined
- 1 cup cooked long grain rice
- ¾ cup shredded Parmesan cheese

1. In a large saucepan, saute mushrooms and garlic in 1 tablespoon oil for 3-4 minutes. Add tomatoes, oregano, sugar, thyme, salt and pepper.

2. Bring to a boil. Reduce heat; cook and simmer for 30 minutes. Uncover; cook 10 minutes longer. Remove from the heat; stir in crab.

3. Meanwhile, in a large skillet, cook scallops and shrimp in remaining oil until shrimp are pink and scallops are opaque.

4. Divide rice among four individual baking dishes. Top with shrimp and scallops. Spoon tomato mixture over seafood and sprinkle with Parmesan cheese. Bake at 350° for 10 minutes or until heated through and cheese is melted.

SEAFOOD IN TOMATO SAUCE

ARTICHOKE SHRIMP BAKE

Scallop Mac & Cheese

Dress up this old standby with seafood. Sweet little bay scallops transform the pasta into a deliciously sophisticated dish.
—LAURIE LUFKIN ESSEX, MA

PREP: 35 MIN. • **BAKE:** 15 MIN.
MAKES: 5 SERVINGS

- 2 cups uncooked medium pasta shells
- ½ cup butter, divided
- 1 cup French bread baguette crumbs
- 1 pound bay scallops
- 1 cup sliced fresh mushrooms
- 1 small onion, chopped
- 3 tablespoons all-purpose flour
- ¾ teaspoon dried thyme
- ¼ teaspoon salt
- ⅛ teaspoon pepper
- 2 cups whole milk
- ½ cup white wine or chicken broth
- 2 tablespoons sherry or chicken broth
- 1 cup (4 ounces) shredded Swiss cheese
- 1 cup (4 ounces) shredded sharp cheddar cheese

1. Cook pasta according to package directions. Meanwhile, in a small skillet, melt 4 tablespoons butter. Add bread crumbs; cook and stir until lightly toasted.
2. In a large skillet over medium heat, melt 2 tablespoons butter. Add scallops; cook and stir for 2 minutes or until firm and opaque. Remove and keep warm. Melt remaining butter in the pan; add mushrooms and onion. Cook and stir until tender. Stir in the flour, thyme, salt and pepper until blended.
3. Gradually add the milk, wine and sherry. Bring to a boil; cook and stir for 1-2 minutes or until thickened. Stir in cheeses until melted. Drain pasta; stir pasta and scallops into sauce.
4. Divide among five 10-oz. ramekins or custard cups. Sprinkle with bread crumbs. Place ramekins on a baking sheet. Bake, uncovered, at 350° for 15-20 minutes or until heated through. Spoon onto plates if desired.

Artichoke Shrimp Bake

You can substitute frozen asparagus cuts for the artichokes and cream of asparagus soup for cream of shrimp in this special-occasion dinner. I usually serve it with rice, but it's also delightful with fresh homemade biscuits.
—JEANNE HOLT MENDOTA HEIGHTS, MN

PREP: 20 MIN. • **BAKE:** 20 MIN.
MAKES: 4 SERVINGS

- 1 pound cooked medium shrimp, peeled and deveined
- 1 can (14 ounces) water-packed artichoke hearts, rinsed, drained and quartered
- ⅔ cup frozen pearl onions, thawed
- 2 cups sliced fresh mushrooms
- 1 small sweet red pepper, chopped
- 2 tablespoons butter
- 1 can (10¾ ounces) condensed cream of shrimp soup, undiluted
- ½ cup sour cream
- ¼ cup sherry or chicken broth
- 2 teaspoons Worcestershire sauce
- 1 teaspoon grated lemon peel
- ⅛ teaspoon white pepper

TOPPING
- ½ cup soft bread crumbs
- ⅓ cup grated Parmesan cheese
- 1 tablespoon minced fresh parsley
- 1 tablespoon butter, melted
    Hot cooked rice, optional

1. Preheat oven to 375°. Place shrimp, artichokes and onions in a greased 11x7-in. baking dish; set aside.
2. In a large skillet, saute mushrooms and red pepper in butter until tender. Stir in soup, sour cream, sherry, Worcestershire sauce, lemon peel and white pepper; heat through. Pour over shrimp mixture.
3. In a small bowl, combine bread crumbs, cheese, parsley and butter; sprinkle over top.
4. Bake, uncovered, 20-25 minutes or until bubbly and topping is golden brown. Serve with rice if desired.

Special Seafood Casserole

I first sampled this casserole at a baby shower and found myself going back for more. The trick is to add a bit of sherry or apple juice to the sauce.

—ANGELA SCHWARTZ MARIETTA, GA

PREP: 25 MIN.
BAKE: 25 MIN. + STANDING
MAKES: 6 SERVINGS

- ½ **pound sea scallops**
- 1 **small onion, finely chopped**
- 1 **celery rib, finely chopped**
- 6 **tablespoons butter, cubed**
- 7 **tablespoons all-purpose flour**
- 1½ **cups half-and-half cream**
- 1 **cup (4 ounces) shredded sharp cheddar cheese**
- 6 **tablespoons sherry or apple juice**
- ¾ **teaspoon salt**
- ¼ **teaspoon cayenne pepper**
- 1 **pound cooked medium shrimp, peeled and deveined**
- 1 **can (6 ounces) crab**
- 1 **can (14 ounces) water-packed artichoke hearts, drained, rinsed, chopped and patted dry**
- 1 **can (8 ounces) sliced water chestnuts, drained**
- ½ **cup sliced almonds**
- ¼ **cup grated Parmesan cheese**

1. Preheat oven to 350°. In a Dutch oven, saute scallops, onion and celery in butter until scallops are firm and opaque. Stir in flour until blended. Add cream. Bring to a boil; cook and stir 2 minutes or until thickened. Reduce heat; add cheddar cheese, sherry, salt and cayenne, stirring until cheese is melted. Remove from heat; set aside.

2. In a greased 11x7-in. baking dish, layer shrimp, crab, artichokes and water chestnuts. Top with sauce. Sprinkle with almonds and Parmesan cheese.

3. Bake, uncovered, 25-30 minutes or until heated through. Let stand 10 minutes before serving.

Lobster Newburg

We live in Maine, so we like to use fresh lobster for these casseroles. But you can also make this recipe with frozen, canned or even imitation lobster.

—**WENDY CORNELL** HUDSON, ME

START TO FINISH: 25 MIN.
MAKES: 4 SERVINGS

- 3 **cups cooked lobster meat or canned flaked lobster meat or imitation lobster chunks**
- 3 **tablespoons butter**
- ¼ **teaspoon paprika**
- 3 **cups heavy whipping cream**
- ½ **teaspoon Worcestershire sauce**
- 3 **egg yolks, lightly beaten**
- 1 **tablespoon sherry, optional**
- ¼ **teaspoon salt**
- ⅓ **cup crushed butter-flavored crackers (about 8 crackers)**

1. In a large skillet, saute the lobster in butter and paprika for 3-4 minutes; set aside. In a large saucepan, bring cream and Worcestershire sauce to a gentle boil. Meanwhile, in a bowl, combine egg yolks, sherry if desired and salt.

2. Remove cream from the heat; stir a small amount into egg yolk mixture. Return all to the pan, stirring constantly. Bring to a gentle boil; cook and stir for 5-7 minutes or until slightly thickened. Stir in the lobster.

3. Divide lobster mixture among four 10-oz. baking dishes. Sprinkle with cracker crumbs. Broil 6 in. from the heat for 2-3 minutes or until golden brown.

TOP TIP

When I have extra time, I'll crush crackers and store them in a labeled, sealed jar. That way, they're on hand when I need them for a recipe or to sprinkle on top of a soup.

—**REGENA J.** LAFAYETTE, IN

SEAFOOD LASAGNA

Seafood Lasagna

I usually serve this casserole on my husband's birthday because it's his favorite. I adapted it from a recipe a friend gave me. I think of it as the crown jewel in my recipe collection.

—**ELENA HANSEN** RUIDOSO, NM

PREP: 35 MIN. • **BAKE:** 35 MIN. + STANDING
MAKES: 12 SERVINGS

- 1 **green onion, finely chopped**
- 2 **tablespoons canola oil**
- 2 **tablespoons plus ½ cup butter, divided**
- ½ **cup chicken broth**
- 1 **bottle (8 ounces) clam juice**
- 1 **pound bay scallops**
- 1 **pound uncooked small shrimp, peeled and deveined**
- 1 **package (8 ounces) imitation crabmeat, chopped**
- ¼ **teaspoon white pepper, divided**
- ½ **cup all-purpose flour**
- 1½ **cups 2% milk**
- ½ **teaspoon salt**
- 1 **cup heavy whipping cream**
- ½ **cup shredded Parmesan cheese, divided**
- 9 **lasagna noodles, cooked and drained**

1. In a large skillet, saute the onion in oil and 2 tablespoons butter until tender. Stir in broth and clam juice; bring to a boil. Add scallops, shrimp, crab and ⅛ teaspoon pepper; return to a boil. Reduce heat; simmer, uncovered, for 4-5 minutes or until shrimp turn pink and scallops are firm and opaque, stirring gently. Drain, reserving cooking liquid; set seafood mixture aside.

2. In a large saucepan, melt the remaining butter; stir in flour until smooth. Combine milk and reserved cooking liquid; gradually add to the saucepan. Add salt and remaining pepper. Bring to a boil; cook and stir for 2 minutes or until thickened.

3. Remove from the heat; stir in cream and ¼ cup cheese. Stir ¾ cup white sauce into the seafood mixture.

4. Preheat oven to 350°. Spread ½ cup white sauce in a greased 13x9-in. baking dish. Top with three noodles; spread with half of the seafood mixture and 1¼ cups sauce. Repeat layers. Top with remaining noodles, sauce and cheese.

5. Bake, uncovered, for 35-40 minutes or until golden brown. Let stand for 15 minutes before cutting.

Spanish-Style Paella

If you enjoy cooking ethnic foods, this hearty rice dish is a great one. It's brimming with generous chunks of sausage, shrimp and veggies.

—TASTE OF HOME COOKING SCHOOL

PREP: 10 MIN. • **COOK:** 35 MIN.
MAKES: 6-8 SERVINGS

- ½ pound bulk Italian sausage
- ½ pound boneless skinless chicken breasts, cubed
- 1 tablespoon olive oil
- 1 garlic clove, minced
- 1 cup uncooked long grain rice
- 1 cup chopped onion
- 1½ cups chicken broth
- 1 can (14½ ounces) stewed tomatoes, undrained
- ½ teaspoon paprika
- ¼ teaspoon ground cayenne pepper
- ¼ teaspoon salt
- 10 strands saffron, crushed or ⅛ teaspoon ground saffron
- ½ pound uncooked medium shrimp, peeled and deveined
- ½ cup sweet red pepper strips
- ½ cup green pepper strips
- ½ cup frozen peas

1. In a large saucepan over medium-high heat, cook sausage and chicken in oil for 5 minutes or until sausage is lightly browned and chicken is no longer pink, stirring frequently. Add garlic; cook 1 minute longer. Drain if necessary.

2. Stir in rice and onion. Cook until onion is tender and rice is lightly browned, stirring frequently. Add the broth, tomatoes, paprika, cayenne, salt and saffron. Bring to a boil. Reduce heat to low; cover and cook for 10 minutes.

3. Stir in the shrimp, peppers and peas. Cover and cook 10 minutes longer or until rice is tender, shrimp turn pink and liquid is absorbed.

Creamy Seafood-Stuffed Shells

Inspired by my love of lasagna, pasta shells and seafood, I came up with a recipe that's a cinch to make but classy enough to serve company. I serve it with garlic bread and a salad for a complete meal.

—KATIE SLOAN CHARLOTTE, NC

PREP: 40 MIN. • **BAKE:** 30 MIN.
MAKES: 8 SERVINGS

- 24 uncooked jumbo pasta shells
- 1 tablespoon finely chopped green pepper
- 1 tablespoon chopped red onion
- 1 teaspoon plus ¼ cup butter, divided
- 2 cans (6 ounces each) lump crabmeat, drained
- 1 package (5 ounces) frozen cooked salad shrimp, thawed
- 1 egg, lightly beaten
- ½ cup shredded part-skim mozzarella cheese
- ¼ cup mayonnaise
- 2 tablespoons plus 4 cups 2% milk, divided
- 1½ teaspoons seafood seasoning, divided
- ¼ teaspoon pepper
- ¼ cup all-purpose flour
- ¼ teaspoon coarsely ground pepper
- 1½ cups grated Parmesan cheese

1. Cook pasta according to package directions.

2. Meanwhile, in a small skillet, saute green pepper and onion in 1 teaspoon butter until tender; set aside.

3. In a large bowl, combine crab, shrimp, egg, mozzarella cheese, mayonnaise, 2 tablespoons milk, 1 teaspoon seafood seasoning, pepper and green pepper mixture.

4. Preheat oven to 350°. Drain and rinse pasta; stuff each shell with 1 rounded tablespoon of seafood mixture. Place in a greased 13x9-in. baking dish.

5. In a small saucepan, melt remaining butter over medium heat. Whisk in flour and coarsely ground pepper; gradually whisk in remaining milk. Bring to a boil; cook and stir 2 minutes or until thickened. Stir in Parmesan cheese.

6. Pour over stuffed shells. Sprinkle with remaining seafood seasoning. Bake, uncovered, 30-35 minutes or until bubbly.

SPANISH-STYLE PAELLA

**MORGAN SEGER'S GRILLED CHEESE
& TOMATO SOUP BAKE** *PAGE 75*

Meatless

GO AHEAD—TRY SOMETHING DIFFERENT!
THESE SAVORY RECIPES ARE SO GOOD, YOU WON'T MISS THE MEAT.

> Yellow squash, zucchini and basil meet ricotta cheese and ravioli in this crowd-pleasing entree with delicious flavors. One bite and you'll know—this is what summer fresh tastes like.
> —TASTE OF HOME TEST KITCHEN

Stacked Vegetables and Ravioli

PREP: 20 MIN. • **BAKE:** 30 MIN. + STANDING
MAKES: 6 SERVINGS

- 2 **yellow summer squash**
- 2 **medium zucchini**
- 1 **package (9 ounces) refrigerated cheese ravioli**
- 1 **cup ricotta cheese**
- 1 **egg**
- ½ **teaspoon garlic salt**
- 1 **jar (24 ounces) marinara or spaghetti sauce**
- 10 **fresh basil leaves, divided**
- ¾ **cup shredded Parmesan cheese**

1. Preheat oven to 350°. Using a vegetable peeler, cut squash and zucchini into very thin lengthwise strips. In a Dutch oven, cook ravioli according to package directions, adding vegetable strips during last 3 minutes of cooking.
2. Meanwhile, in a small bowl, combine ricotta cheese, egg and garlic salt; set aside. Drain ravioli and vegetables.
3. Spread ½ cup marinara sauce into a greased 11x7-in. baking dish. Layer with half the ravioli and vegetables, half the ricotta mixture, seven basil leaves and 1 cup marinara sauce. Layer with remaining ravioli, vegetables and marinara sauce. Dollop remaining ricotta mixture over top; sprinkle with Parmesan cheese.
4. Cover and bake 25 minutes. Uncover and bake 5-10 minutes longer or until cheese is melted. Let stand 10 minutes before cutting. Thinly slice remaining basil; sprinkle over top.

STACKED VEGETABLES AND RAVIOLI

Upside-Down Meatless Pizza

I experimented with a recipe for upside-down pizza and made it into a meatless dish. The result was very tasty.

—**MARIE FIGUEROA** WAUWATOSA, WI

PREP: 25 MIN. • **BAKE:** 20 MIN.
MAKES: 8 SERVINGS

- 1 **small onion, chopped**
- ¼ **cup chopped green pepper**
- 3 **tablespoons canola oil, divided**
- 2 **tablespoons plus 1 cup all-purpose flour, divided**
- ½ **teaspoon dried basil**
- ½ **teaspoon fennel seed**
- 1 **package (10 ounces) frozen chopped spinach, thawed and squeezed dry**
- 1 **cup sliced fresh mushrooms**
- 1 **can (15 ounces) tomato sauce**
- 2 **cups (8 ounces) shredded cheddar cheese**
- 2 **eggs**
- ¾ **cup 2% milk**
- ½ **teaspoon salt**
- 2 **tablespoons grated Parmesan cheese**

1. Preheat oven to 425°. In a large skillet, saute onion and green pepper in 2 tablespoons oil until tender. Stir in 2 tablespoons flour, basil and fennel until blended. Add the spinach, mushrooms and tomato sauce. Bring to a boil; cook and stir 2 minutes or until thickened.

2. Pour into a greased 11x7-in. baking dish. Sprinkle with cheddar cheese. Place the remaining flour in a large bowl. Add eggs, milk, salt and remaining oil; beat until smooth. Stir in Parmesan cheese. Pour over vegetable mixture.

3. Bake, uncovered, 20-25 minutes or until a thermometer reads 160°.

TOP TIP

My husband doesn't like green peppers, so when a recipe calls for them, I use fresh snow peas from my garden instead. Snow peas freeze well, too.

—**GINNY BARKMAN** CHASE, BC

TORTELLINI SPINACH CASSEROLE

Tortellini Spinach Casserole

This casserole's wonderful taste will delight even those who say they don't like spinach. In fact, people are often surprised at just how good it is! Whenever I bring it to a gathering, it doesn't last long.

—**BARBARA KELLEN** ANTIOCH, IL

PREP: 20 MIN. • **BAKE:** 20 MIN.
MAKES: 12 SERVINGS

- 1 **package (19 ounces) frozen cheese tortellini**
- 1 **pound sliced fresh mushrooms**
- 1 **teaspoon garlic powder**
- ¼ **teaspoon onion powder**
- ¼ **teaspoon pepper**
- ½ **cup butter, divided**
- 1 **can (12 ounces) evaporated milk**
- ½ **pound brick cheese, cubed**
- 3 **packages (10 ounces each) frozen chopped spinach, thawed and squeezed dry**
- 2 **cups (8 ounces) shredded part-skim mozzarella cheese**

1. Preheat oven to 350°. Cook tortellini according to package directions.

2. Meanwhile, in a large skillet, saute mushrooms, garlic powder, onion powder and pepper in ¼ cup butter until mushrooms are tender. Remove and keep warm.

3. In the same skillet, combine milk and remaining butter. Bring to a gentle boil; stir in brick cheese until smooth. Drain tortellini; place in a large bowl. Stir in mushroom mixture and spinach. Add cheese sauce and toss to coat.

4. Transfer to a greased 13x9-in. baking dish; sprinkle with mozzarella cheese. Cover and bake 15 minutes. Uncover; bake 5-10 minutes longer or until heated through and the cheese is melted.

Portobello Spaghetti Casserole

You can't go wrong with this easy, Italian-style casserole. Substitute shiitakes or plain button mushrooms for the portobellos, if you prefer.

—MARY SHIVERS ADA, OK

PREP: 30 MIN. • **BAKE:** 40 MIN.
MAKES: 3 SERVINGS

- 4 **ounces uncooked spaghetti**
- 3 **portobello mushrooms, stems removed and thinly sliced**
- ¼ **teaspoon salt**
- ⅛ **teaspoon pepper**
- 1 **tablespoon olive oil**
- 1 **egg**
- ¼ **cup sour cream**
- 2 **tablespoons grated Parmesan cheese**
- 1 **tablespoon minced fresh parsley**
- 1½ **teaspoons all-purpose flour**
- ¼ **teaspoon garlic powder**
- ⅛ **teaspoon crushed red pepper flakes**
- 1¼ **cups marinara sauce**
- ¾ **cup shredded part-skim mozzarella cheese**

1. Cook spaghetti according to package directions. Meanwhile, in a large skillet, saute the mushrooms, salt and pepper in oil until the mushrooms are tender; drain.
2. In a large bowl, combine the egg, sour cream, Parmesan cheese, parsley, flour, garlic powder and pepper flakes. Drain spaghetti; add to sour cream mixture.
3. Transfer to a 1½-qt. baking dish coated with cooking spray. Top with mushrooms and marinara sauce.
4. Cover and bake at 350° for 30 minutes. Uncover; sprinkle with the mozzarella cheese. Bake 10-15 minutes longer or until a thermometer reads 160° and cheese is melted. Let stand 10 minutes before serving.

SWEET POTATO CHILI BAKE

Sweet Potato Chili Bake

I'm a vegetarian and wanted to develop some dishes that are a little heartier than traditional vegetarian fare. Here's one that's very satisfying!

—JILLIAN TOURNOUX MASSILLON, OH

PREP: 30 MIN. • **BAKE:** 20 MIN.
MAKES: 7 SERVINGS

- 2 **cups cubed peeled sweet potato**
- 1 **medium sweet red pepper, chopped**
- 1 **tablespoon olive oil**
- 1 **garlic clove, minced**
- 1 **can (28 ounces) diced tomatoes, undrained**
- 2 **cups vegetable broth**
- 1 **can (15 ounces) black beans, rinsed and drained**
- 4½ **teaspoons brown sugar**
- 3 **teaspoons chili powder**
- 1 **teaspoon salt**
- ½ **teaspoon pepper**
- 1 **package (6½ ounces) corn bread/muffin mix**
- ½ **cup shredded cheddar cheese**
  Optional toppings: sour cream, shredded cheddar cheese and chopped seeded jalapeno pepper

1. In an ovenproof Dutch oven, saute sweet potato and red pepper in oil until crisp-tender. Add garlic; cook 1 minute longer. Add tomatoes, broth, beans, brown sugar, chili powder, salt and pepper. Bring to a boil. Reduce heat; simmer, uncovered, 15-20 minutes or until potatoes are tender.
2. Meanwhile, preheat oven to 400°. Prepare corn bread batter according to package directions; stir in cheese. Drop by tablespoonfuls over chili.
3. Cover and bake 18-20 minutes or until a toothpick inserted in center comes out clean. Serve with toppings of your choice.
NOTE *Wear disposable gloves when cutting hot peppers; the oils can burn skin. Avoid touching your face.*

TOP TIP

Select sweet potatoes that are firm, with no cracks or bruises. To keep them fresh for up to 2 weeks, store in a cool, dark, well-ventilated place; if the temperature is above 60°, they'll sprout faster.

Grilled Cheese & Tomato Soup Bake

This casserole brings together two classic comfort foods, grilled cheese sandwiches and tomato soup, with no dipping or dunking required. Even my picky-eater husband devours it.
—**MORGAN SEGER** ANSONIA, OH

PREP: 25 MIN. • **BAKE:** 25 MIN. + STANDING
MAKES: 6 SERVINGS

- 3 ounces reduced-fat cream cheese
- 1½ teaspoons dried basil, divided
- 12 slices Italian, sourdough or rye bread (½ inch thick)
- 6 slices part-skim mozzarella cheese
- 6 tablespoons butter, softened
- ½ cup tomato paste
- 1 garlic clove, minced
- ¼ teaspoon salt
- ¼ teaspoon pepper
- 1¾ cups 2% milk
- 2 eggs
- 1 cup (4 ounces) shredded Italian cheese blend or part-skim mozzarella cheese

1. Preheat oven to 350°. In a small bowl, mix cream cheese and 1 teaspoon basil until blended; spread onto six bread slices. Top with mozzarella cheese and remaining bread. Spread outsides of sandwiches with butter. Arrange in a greased 13x9-in. baking dish.

2. In a small saucepan, combine tomato paste, garlic, salt, pepper and remaining basil; cook and stir over medium heat 1 minute. Gradually whisk in milk; bring to a boil. Reduce heat; simmer, uncovered, 4-5 minutes or until thickened, stirring frequently. Remove from heat.

3. Whisk eggs in a large bowl; gradually whisk in a third of the milk mixture. Stir in remaining milk mixture; pour over sandwiches. Sprinkle with Italian cheese blend.

4. Bake, uncovered, 25-30 minutes or until golden brown and cheese is melted. Let stand 10 minutes before serving.

Southwest Vegetarian Bake

This veggie-packed casserole hits the spot on chilly nights. It's also great any time I have a craving for Mexican food with all the fixings.
—**PATRICIA GALE** MONTICELLO, IL

PREP: 40 MIN. • **BAKE:** 35 MIN. + STANDING
MAKES: 8 SERVINGS

- ¾ cup uncooked brown rice
- 1½ cups water
- 1 can (15 ounces) black beans, rinsed and drained
- 1 can (11 ounces) Mexicorn, drained
- 1 can (10 ounces) diced tomatoes and green chilies
- 1 cup salsa
- 1 cup (8 ounces) reduced-fat sour cream
- 1 cup (4 ounces) shredded reduced-fat cheddar cheese
- ¼ teaspoon pepper
- ½ cup chopped red onion
- 1 can (2¼ ounces) sliced ripe olives, drained
- 1 cup (4 ounces) shredded reduced-fat Mexican cheese blend

1. In a large saucepan, bring rice and water to a boil. Reduce heat; cover and simmer 35-40 minutes or until tender. Preheat oven to 350°. In a large bowl, combine beans, Mexicorn, tomatoes, salsa, sour cream, cheddar cheese, pepper and rice. Transfer to a shallow 2½-qt. baking dish coated with cooking spray. Sprinkle with onion and olives.

2. Bake, uncovered, 30 minutes. Sprinkle with Mexican cheese. Bake 5-10 minutes or until heated through and cheese is melted. Let stand 10 minutes before serving.

**GRILLED CHEESE &
TOMATO SOUP BAKE**

FREEZE IT
Make-Ahead Spinach Manicotti

When I invite people to dinner, many have started requesting this pasta bake ahead of time. It's that good! Plus, the manicotti is stuffed before it's cooked, making it even more convenient for your mealtime planning.

—CHRISTY FREEMAN CENTRAL POINT, OR

PREP: 20 MIN. + CHILLING • **BAKE:** 40 MIN.
MAKES: 7 SERVINGS

- 1 carton (15 ounces) whole-milk ricotta cheese
- 1 package (10 ounces) frozen chopped spinach, thawed and squeezed dry
- 1½ cups (6 ounces) shredded part-skim mozzarella cheese, divided
- ¾ cup shredded Parmesan cheese, divided
- 1 egg, lightly beaten
- 2 teaspoons minced fresh parsley
- ½ teaspoon onion powder
- ½ teaspoon pepper
- ⅛ teaspoon garlic powder
- 3 jars (24 ounces each) spaghetti sauce
- 1 cup water
- 1 package (8 ounces) manicotti shells

1. In a large bowl, mix ricotta, spinach, 1 cup mozzarella cheese, ¼ cup Parmesan cheese, egg, parsley and seasonings. In a large bowl, mix the spaghetti sauce and water; spread 1 cup into a greased 13x9-in. baking dish.

2. Fill uncooked manicotti shells with ricotta mixture; arrange over sauce. Pour remaining spaghetti sauce mixture over top. Sprinkle with remaining mozzarella cheese and Parmesan cheese. Refrigerate, covered, overnight.

3. Remove from the refrigerator 30 minutes before baking. Preheat oven to 350°. Bake, uncovered, 40-50 minutes or until manicotti is tender.

FREEZE OPTION *Cover and freeze unbaked casserole. To use, partially thaw in refrigerator overnight. Remove from refrigerator 30 minutes before baking. Preheat oven to 350°. Bake casserole as directed, increasing time as necessary to heat through and for a thermometer inserted in center to read 165°.*

⅛ teaspoon salt
⅛ teaspoon ground cumin
¾ cup salsa
2 tablespoons minced fresh cilantro
3 corn tortillas (6 inches)
¾ cup shredded cheddar cheese
  Sour cream, optional

1. In a large skillet, saute zucchini and pepper in oil until pepper is crisp-tender. Add garlic; cook 1 minute longer. Add the corn, beans, salt and cumin; saute 2-3 minutes longer. Stir in salsa and cilantro.

2. Place a tortilla in the bottom of a 1½-qt. round baking dish coated with cooking spray. Spread with ⅔ cup of the vegetable mixture; sprinkle with ¼ cup cheese. Repeat layers twice.

3. Bake, uncovered, at 350° for 20-25 minutes or until heated through and the cheese is melted. Let stand for 10 minutes before serving. Serve with sour cream if desired.

Black Bean Nacho Bake

Pasta, black beans and nacho cheese soup combine in this speedy six-ingredient supper. Top individual servings with cheddar cheese and crunchy tortilla chips.
—**MELODIE GAY** SALT LAKE CITY, UT

PREP: 15 MIN. • **BAKE:** 30 MIN.
MAKES: 4 SERVINGS

1 package (7 ounces) small pasta shells, cooked and drained
1 can (15 ounces) black beans, rinsed and drained
1 can (11 ounces) condensed nacho cheese soup, undiluted
⅓ cup 2% milk
½ cup crushed tortilla chips
½ cup shredded cheddar cheese

1. Preheat oven to 350°. In a large bowl, combine pasta and beans. In a small bowl, combine soup and milk; stir into macaroni mixture.

2. Transfer to a greased 8-in.-square baking dish. Cover and bake 25 minutes. Uncover; sprinkle with tortilla chips and cheese. Bake 5-10 minutes longer or until pasta is tender and cheese is melted.

Black-Eyed Peas 'n' Pasta

Tradition has it that if you eat black-eyed peas on New Year's Day, you'll enjoy prosperity all year through. But I serve this tasty combination of pasta, peas and tangy tomatoes any time.
—**MARIE MALSCH** BRIDGMAN, MI

START TO FINISH: 30 MIN.
MAKES: 6 SERVINGS

1 cup chopped green pepper
½ cup chopped onion
1 jalapeno pepper, seeded and chopped
3 garlic cloves, minced
1 tablespoon olive oil
1 can (28 ounces) crushed tomatoes
1 can (15½ ounces) black-eyed peas, rinsed and drained
1 to 3 tablespoons minced fresh cilantro
1 teaspoon cider vinegar
1 teaspoon sugar
1 teaspoon salt
⅛ teaspoon pepper
5 cups hot cooked bow tie pasta

1. Saute the green pepper, onion, jalapeno and garlic in oil in a large skillet for 5 minutes or until tender. Add tomatoes; bring to a boil. Simmer, uncovered, for 10 minutes.

2. Stir in peas, cilantro, vinegar, sugar, salt and pepper; simmer 10 minutes longer. Toss with pasta.

NOTE *Wear disposable gloves when cutting hot peppers; the oils can burn skin. Avoid touching your face.*

Vegetarian Enchilada Bake

I've had this budget-friendly vegetarian recipe for years. You'll enjoy the delicious Tex-Mex flavors, even without the meat!
—**BARBARA STELLUTO** DEVON, PA

PREP: 20 MIN. • **BAKE:** 20 MIN. + STANDING
MAKES: 3 SERVINGS

1 cup shredded zucchini
1 tablespoon finely chopped sweet red pepper
1 teaspoon olive oil
1 garlic clove, minced
¾ cup frozen corn
¾ cup black beans, rinsed and drained

CORN BREAD-
TOPPED FRIJOLES

Corn Bread-Topped Frijoles

My family often asks for this economical slow-cooker favorite. It's loaded with Southwestern flavors.

—SUZANNE CALDWELL ARTESIA, NM

PREP: 20 MIN. • **COOK:** 3 HOURS
MAKES: 8 SERVINGS

- 1 medium onion, chopped
- 1 medium green pepper, chopped
- 1 tablespoon canola oil
- 2 garlic cloves, minced
- 1 can (16 ounces) kidney beans, rinsed and drained
- 1 can (15 ounces) pinto beans, rinsed and drained
- 1 can (14½ ounces) diced tomatoes, undrained
- 1 can (8 ounces) tomato sauce
- 1 teaspoon chili powder
- ½ teaspoon pepper
- ⅛ teaspoon hot pepper sauce

CORN BREAD TOPPING

- 1 cup all-purpose flour
- 1 cup yellow cornmeal
- 1 tablespoon sugar
- 1½ teaspoons baking powder
- ½ teaspoon salt
- 2 eggs, lightly beaten
- 1¼ cups fat-free milk
- 1 can (8¾ ounces) cream-style corn
- 3 tablespoons canola oil

1. In a large skillet, saute onion and green pepper in oil until tender. Add garlic; cook 1 minute longer. Transfer to a greased 5-qt. slow cooker.
2. Stir in the beans, tomatoes, tomato sauce, chili powder, pepper and pepper sauce. Cover and cook on high for 1 hour.
3. In a large bowl, combine the flour, cornmeal, sugar, baking powder and salt. Combine the eggs, milk, corn and oil; add to dry ingredients and mix well. Spoon evenly over bean mixture.
4. Cover and cook on high for 2 hours or until a toothpick inserted near the center of corn bread comes out clean.

FAST FIX
Confetti Mac 'n' Cheese

The cheese disguises the zucchini in this dish, so my kids keep on eating it! My family loves this rich dinner option.

—DEBBIE AMACHER AMHERST, NY

START TO FINISH: 25 MIN.
MAKES: 4 SERVINGS

- 1½ cups uncooked elbow macaroni
- 2 cups chopped zucchini
- ½ cup chopped onion
- 2 tablespoons canola oil
- 1 can (14½ ounces) diced tomatoes, drained
- 1 can (10¾ ounces) condensed cheddar cheese soup, undiluted
- 2 cups (8 ounces) shredded cheddar cheese
- ½ cup milk
- ½ teaspoon dried basil
- ½ teaspoon prepared mustard

1. Cook macaroni according to package directions. Meanwhile, in a large saucepan, saute zucchini and onion in oil until tender. Stir in the tomatoes, soup, cheese, milk, basil and mustard.
2. Cook, uncovered, over medium heat for 6-7 minutes or until the cheese is melted, stirring often. Drain macaroni; toss with the vegetable cheese sauce.

Provolone Ziti Bake

As simple as it is delicious, this Italian meal appeals to everyone. Serve with salad and hot French bread, and watch it disappear.

—VICKY PALMER ALBUQUERQUE, NM

PREP: 20 MIN. • **BAKE:** 65 MIN.
MAKES: 8 SERVINGS

- 1 tablespoon olive oil
- 1 medium onion, chopped
- 3 garlic cloves, minced
- 2 cans (28 ounces each) Italian crushed tomatoes
- 1½ cups water
- ½ cup dry red wine or reduced-sodium chicken broth
- 1 tablespoon sugar
- 1 teaspoon dried basil
- 1 package (16 ounces) ziti or small tube pasta
- 8 slices provolone cheese

1. Preheat oven to 350°. In a 6-qt. stockpot, heat oil over medium-high heat. Add onion; cook and stir 3-4 minutes or until tender. Add garlic; cook 1 minute longer. Stir in tomatoes, water, wine, sugar and basil. Bring to a boil; remove from heat. Stir in ziti.
2. Transfer to a 13x9-in. baking dish coated with cooking spray. Bake, covered, 1 hour. Top with cheese. Bake, uncovered, 4-6 minutes longer or until ziti is tender and cheese is melted.

Vegetarian Potato au Gratin

Load up on veggies when you serve this appetizing casserole. You'll appreciate the homey bread-crumb topping and hands-free bake time at the end of the day. What could be better?

—TASTE OF HOME TEST KITCHEN

PREP: 15 MIN. • **BAKE:** 50 MIN. + STANDING
MAKES: 6 SERVINGS

- 3 medium carrots, thinly sliced
- 1 medium green pepper, chopped
- 4 tablespoons butter, divided
- 3 tablespoons all-purpose flour
- 1 teaspoon dried oregano
- ½ teaspoon salt
- 2½ cups 2% milk
- 1 can (15 ounces) black beans, rinsed and drained
- 3 cups (12 ounces) shredded Swiss cheese, divided
- 4 medium Yukon Gold potatoes, thinly sliced
- ½ cup seasoned bread crumbs

1. Preheat oven to 400°. In a large saucepan, saute the carrots and pepper in 3 tablespoons butter until tender. Stir in flour, oregano and salt until blended; gradually add milk. Bring to a boil; cook and stir 2 minutes or until thickened. Stir in beans and 2 cups cheese until cheese is melted.
2. Layer half of the potatoes and sauce in a greased 13x9-in. baking dish; repeat layers. Sprinkle with remaining cheese. In a microwave, melt the remaining butter. Stir in bread crumbs. Sprinkle over top.
3. Cover and bake 50-55 minutes. Let stand 10 minutes before serving.

Hearty Tomato-Olive Penne

Who needs meat when you have a pasta dish loaded with tomatoes, olives and Havarti cheese? I often assemble it in advance and bake it the next day, adding just a few minutes to the cooking time.

—JACQUELINE FRANK GREEN BAY, WI

PREP: 50 MIN. • **BAKE:** 25 MIN.
MAKES: 8 SERVINGS

- 2 large onions, chopped
- 6 tablespoons olive oil
- 3 garlic cloves, minced
- 3 pounds plum tomatoes, seeded and chopped (about 10 tomatoes)
- 1 cup vegetable broth
- 1 tablespoon dried basil
- 1 teaspoon crushed red pepper flakes
- ½ teaspoon salt
- ¼ teaspoon pepper
- 1 package (16 ounces) uncooked penne pasta
- 1 block (24 ounces) Havarti cheese, cut into ½-in. cubes
- 1 cup pitted Greek olives
- ⅓ cup grated Parmesan cheese

1. In a Dutch oven, saute onions in oil until tender. Add garlic; cook 1 minute longer. Stir in tomatoes, broth, basil, pepper flakes, salt and pepper. Bring to a boil. Reduce heat; cover and simmer 25-30 minutes or until sauce is slightly thickened.
2. Meanwhile, cook penne according to package directions; drain.
3. Preheat oven to 375°. Stir Havarti cheese, olives and cooked penne into the sauce. Transfer to a greased 13x9-in. baking dish; sprinkle with Parmesan cheese.
4. Cover and bake 20 minutes. Uncover; bake 5 minutes longer or until cheese is melted.

THE BEST EGGPLANT PARMESAN

Vegetarian Tex-Mex Peppers

Folks who enjoy stuffed peppers will love this twist on the recipe. The filling holds together well and has a good amount of heat to counter the peppers' sweetness.

—**CELE KNIGHT** NACOGDOCHES, TX

PREP: 20 MIN. • **BAKE:** 45 MIN.
MAKES: 4 SERVINGS

- 4 **large green peppers**
- 2 **eggs, beaten**
- 2 **cups cooked brown rice**
- 1 **cup frozen vegetarian meat crumbles**
- 1 **cup canned black beans, rinsed and drained**
- ½ **teaspoon pepper**
- ¼ **teaspoon hot pepper sauce**
- ¼ **teaspoon ground cardamom, optional**
- 1 **can (14½ ounces) diced tomatoes, drained**
- 1 **can (10 ounces) diced tomatoes and green chilies**
- 1 **can (8 ounces) no-salt-added tomato sauce**
- ½ **cup shredded Colby cheese**

1. Preheat oven to 350°. Cut the peppers in half lengthwise and remove seeds. Discard stems. In a Dutch oven, cook peppers in boiling water 3-5 minutes. Drain and rinse in cold water; set aside.

2. In a large bowl, combine eggs, rice, meat crumbles, beans, pepper, pepper sauce and, if desired, cardamom. Spoon into peppers. Place in a 13x9-in. baking dish coated with cooking spray.

3. In a small bowl, combine diced tomatoes, tomatoes and green chilies, and tomato sauce. Spoon over peppers. Cover and bake 40-45 minutes or until a thermometer reads 160°. Sprinkle with cheese; bake 5 minutes longer or until cheese is melted.

NOTE *Vegetarian meat crumbles are a nutritious protein source made from soy. Look for them in the natural foods freezer section.*

The Best Eggplant Parmesan

I love eggplant and have many recipes that include it, but this one is my favorite. The cheeses and seasonings make this dish unforgettable.

—**DOTTIE KILPATRICK** WILMINGTON, NC

PREP: 1¼ HOURS
BAKE: 35 MIN. + STANDING
MAKES: 2 CASSEROLES (8 SERVINGS EACH)

- 3 **garlic cloves, minced**
- ⅓ **cup olive oil**
- 2 **cans (28 ounces each) crushed tomatoes**
- 1 **cup pitted ripe olives, chopped**
- ¼ **cup thinly sliced fresh basil leaves or 1 tablespoon dried basil**
- 3 **tablespoons capers, drained**
- 1 **teaspoon crushed red pepper flakes**
- ¼ **teaspoon pepper**

EGGPLANT
- 1 **cup all-purpose flour**
- 4 **eggs, beaten**
- 3 **cups dry bread crumbs**
- 1 **tablespoon garlic powder**
- 1 **tablespoon minced fresh oregano or 1 teaspoon dried oregano**
- 4 **small eggplants (about 1 pound each), peeled and cut lengthwise into ½-inch slices**
- 1 **cup olive oil**

CHEESE
- 2 **eggs, beaten**
- 2 **cartons (15 ounces each) ricotta cheese**

- 1¼ **cups shredded Parmesan cheese, divided**
- ½ **cup thinly sliced fresh basil leaves or 2 tablespoons dried basil**
- ½ **teaspoon pepper**
- 8 **cups (32 ounces) shredded part-skim mozzarella cheese**

1. In a Dutch oven over medium heat, cook garlic in oil 1 minute. Stir in tomatoes, olives, basil, capers, pepper flakes and pepper. Bring to a boil. Reduce heat; simmer, uncovered, 45-60 minutes or until thickened.

2. Meanwhile, for eggplant, place flour and eggs in separate shallow bowls. In another bowl, combine bread crumbs, garlic powder and oregano. Dip eggplant in flour, eggs, then bread crumb mixture.

3. In a large skillet, cook eggplant in batches in oil for 5 minutes on each side or until tender. Drain on paper towels. In a large bowl, combine the eggs, ricotta, ½ cup Parmesan cheese, basil and pepper.

4. Preheat oven to 350°. In each of two greased 13x9-in. baking dishes, layer 1½ cups tomato sauce, four eggplant slices, 1 cup ricotta mixture and 2 cups mozzarella cheese. Repeat layers. Sprinkle each with remaining Parmesan cheese. Bake, uncovered, 35-40 minutes or until bubbly. Let stand 10 minutes before cutting.

Greek Zucchini & Feta Bake

Looking for a main dish that's light, indulgent and golden on top? Turn to this delicious Greek-style bake.

—GABRIELA STEFANESCU WEBSTER, TX

PREP: 40 MIN. • **BAKE:** 30 MIN. + STANDING
MAKES: 12 SERVINGS

- 2 tablespoons olive oil, divided
- 5 medium zucchini, cut into ½-in. cubes (about 6 cups)
- 2 large onions, chopped (about 4 cups)
- 1 teaspoon dried oregano, divided
- ½ teaspoon salt
- ¼ teaspoon pepper
- 6 eggs
- 2 teaspoons baking powder
- 1 cup (8 ounces) reduced-fat plain yogurt
- 1 cup all-purpose flour
- 2 packages (8 ounces each) feta cheese, cubed
- ¼ cup minced fresh parsley
- 1 teaspoon paprika

1. Preheat oven to 350°. In a Dutch oven, heat 1 tablespoon oil over medium-high heat. Add half of the zucchini, half of the onions and ½ teaspoon oregano; cook and stir 8-10 minutes or until zucchini is crisp-tender. Remove from pan. Repeat with remaining vegetables. Stir in salt and pepper. Cool slightly.

2. In a large bowl, whisk eggs and baking powder until blended; whisk in yogurt and flour just until blended. Stir in cheese, parsley and zucchini mixture. Transfer to a greased 13x9-in. baking dish. Sprinkle with paprika.

3. Bake, uncovered, 30-35 minutes or until golden brown and set. Let stand 10 minutes before cutting.

NOTE *If desired, thinly slice 1 medium zucchini and toss with 2 teaspoons olive oil; arrange over casserole before sprinkling with paprika. Bake as directed.*

GREEK ZUCCHINI & FETA BAKE

**VICKI ANDERSON'S PROSCIUTTO-
PESTO BREAKFAST STRATA** PAGE 93

Breakfast

BREAKFAST IS THE IMPORTANT MEAL OF THE DAY!
RISE AND SHINE TO THESE SUNNY DISHES.

**LAURI KNOX'S GREEK
BREAKFAST CASSEROLE**
PAGE 91

**SHARON RICCI'S ORANGE
BREAKFAST SOUFFLE WITH
DRIED CHERRIES** PAGE 93

**NANCY ZIMMERMAN'S
BANANA FRENCH TOAST BAKE**
PAGE 86

RAISIN BREAD & SAUSAGE MORNING CASSEROLE

Raisin Bread & Sausage Morning Casserole

When we used to have Sunday breakfasts with my grandparents, my mom often made this for my grandpa because he enjoyed it so much. Pork sausage and cinnamon bread taste surprisingly good together here.

—**CAROLYN LEVAN** DIXON, IL

PREP: 25 MIN. + CHILLING • **BAKE:** 35 MIN.
MAKES: 12 SERVINGS

- ½ **pound bulk pork sausage**
- 1 **loaf (1 pound) cinnamon-raisin bread, cubed**
- 6 **eggs**
- 1½ **cups 2% milk**
- 1½ **cups half-and-half cream**
- 1 **teaspoon vanilla extract**
- ¼ **teaspoon ground cinnamon**
- ¼ **teaspoon ground nutmeg**

TOPPING
- 1 **cup chopped pecans**
- 1 **cup packed brown sugar**
- ½ **cup butter, softened**
- 2 **tablespoons maple syrup**

1. In a large skillet, cook sausage over medium heat 4-6 minutes or until no longer pink, breaking into crumbles; drain. In a greased 13x9-in. baking dish, combine bread and sausage.

2. In a large bowl, whisk the eggs, milk, cream, vanilla, cinnamon and nutmeg until blended; pour over bread. Refrigerate, covered, several hours or overnight.

3. Preheat oven to 350°. Remove casserole from refrigerator while oven heats. In a small bowl, beat topping ingredients until blended. Drop by tablespoonfuls over casserole.

4. Bake, uncovered, 35-45 minutes or until golden brown and a knife inserted near the center comes out clean. Let stand 5-10 minutes before serving.

Eggs Benedict Bake with Bearnaise Sauce

I've made this recipe for my family every Christmas morning for 10 years—it's a holiday tradition that we always look forward to, though it's just as good any other time of the year. Part of what makes it special are the croissants, which help to give it a light, fluffy texture.

—SUSAN TRIPLETT CITRUS HEIGHTS, CA

PREP: 20 MIN. + CHILLING • **BAKE:** 45 MIN.
MAKES: 12 SERVINGS

- ¾ pound Canadian bacon
- 6 croissants, cut into ½-inch cubes
- 10 eggs
- 2 cups 2% milk
- 3 green onions, chopped
- 1 teaspoon onion powder
- 1 teaspoon ground mustard
- 1 teaspoon dried tarragon
- ½ teaspoon salt
- ½ teaspoon white pepper
- ½ teaspoon paprika
- 1 envelope bearnaise sauce

1. Place half of the Canadian bacon in a greased 13x9-in. baking dish. Layer with croissants and remaining Canadian bacon. In a large bowl, whisk eggs, milk, green onions, onion powder, mustard, tarragon, salt and pepper until blended; pour over top. Sprinkle with paprika. Refrigerate, covered, several hours or overnight.
2. Preheat oven to 375°. Remove casserole from refrigerator while oven heats. Bake, covered, 30 minutes. Bake, uncovered, 15-20 minutes longer or until a knife inserted near the center comes out clean. Let stand 5-10 minutes before serving.
3. Prepare sauce according to package directions. Serve with casserole.

FAST FIX ▶

Bacon Swiss Squares

Not only does this scrumptious breakfast pizza come together easily, but it's a cinch to double the ingredients when I'm cooking for an extra-large event. Biscuit mix makes it convenient, and the combination of eggs, bacon and Swiss cheese keeps guests coming back for second helpings.

—AGARITA VAUGHAN FAIRBURY, IL

START TO FINISH: 30 MIN.
MAKES: 12 SERVINGS

- 2 cups biscuit/baking mix
- ½ cup cold water
- 8 ounces sliced Swiss cheese
- 1 pound sliced bacon, cooked and crumbled
- 4 eggs, lightly beaten
- ¼ cup milk
- ½ teaspoon onion powder

1. In a large bowl, combine the biscuit mix and water. Turn onto a floured surface; knead 10 times. Roll into a 14x10-in. rectangle.
2. Place on the bottom and ½ in. up the sides of a greased 13x9-in. baking dish. Arrange cheese over dough. Sprinkle with bacon. In a large bowl, whisk eggs, milk and onion powder; pour over bacon.
3. Bake at 425° for 15-18 minutes or until a knife inserted near the center comes out clean. Cut into squares; serve immediately.

Ham & Cheese Egg Bake

Sure, this delectable dish is a comforting and convenient option for breakfast, but it's just as good for lunch or dinner.

—LISA RENSHAW KANSAS CITY, MO

PREP: 15 MIN. • **BAKE:** 25 MIN.
MAKES: 6 SERVINGS

- 5 eggs
- ¼ cup all-purpose flour
- ½ teaspoon baking powder
- 2 cups (8 ounces) shredded Havarti cheese
- 1 cup (4 ounces) shredded Swiss cheese
- 1 cup cubed fully cooked ham
- 1 cup ricotta cheese
- ¼ cup butter, melted
- 2 tablespoons snipped fresh dill or 2 teaspoons dill weed
- 2 tablespoons Dijon mustard
- ½ teaspoon fennel seed

1. In a large bowl, beat eggs on medium-high speed for 2 minutes or until lemon-colored. Combine flour and baking powder; gradually add to eggs and mix well. Stir in remaining ingredients.
2. Pour into a greased 11x7-in. baking dish. Bake, uncovered, at 375° for 24-28 minutes or until a knife inserted near the center comes out clean. Let stand for 5 minutes before cutting.

BACON SWISS SQUARES

Hash Brown & Chicken Brunch Casserole

Piping hot breakfasts are difficult to put together with two little ones at home. But this egg bake is so easy, we have it all the time. Also, it disappears in a flash whenever I bring it to work.

—JENNIFER BERRY LEXINGTON, OH

PREP: 20 MIN. + CHILLING
BAKE: 1¼ HOURS
MAKES: 12 SERVINGS

- 15 **eggs, beaten**
- 1 **package (28 ounces) frozen O'Brien potatoes**
- 1 **rotisserie chicken, skin removed, shredded**
- 1½ **cups 2% milk**
- 1 **can (10 ounces) diced tomatoes and green chilies, undrained**
- 2 **cups (8 ounces) shredded cheddar cheese, divided**
- 5 **green onions, chopped**
- 3 **tablespoons minced fresh cilantro**
- 1 **teaspoon ground cumin**
- 1½ **teaspoons salt**
- ½ **teaspoon pepper**

1. In a very large bowl, combine eggs, potatoes, chicken, milk, tomatoes, 1 cup cheese, green onions, cilantro and seasonings until blended. Transfer to a greased 13x9-in. baking dish; sprinkle with remaining cheese. Refrigerate, covered, several hours or overnight.

2. Preheat oven to 350°. Remove casserole from refrigerator while oven heats. Bake, uncovered, 1¼ to 1½ hours or until golden brown and a knife inserted near the center comes out clean. Let stand 5-10 minutes before serving.

BANANA FRENCH TOAST BAKE

Banana French Toast Bake

Hamburger buns and bananas come together in this whimsical make-ahead dish the whole family will love. It's the ultimate breakfast for dinner.

—NANCY ZIMMERMAN
CAPE MAY COURT HOUSE, NJ

PREP: 20 MIN. + CHILLING
BAKE: 55 MIN. + STANDING
MAKES: 8 SERVINGS

- 6 **whole wheat hamburger buns**
- 1 **package (8 ounces) reduced-fat cream cheese, cut into ¾-inch cubes**
- 3 **medium bananas, sliced**
- 6 **eggs**
- 4 **cups fat-free milk**
- ¼ **cup sugar**
- ¼ **cup maple syrup**
- ½ **teaspoon ground cinnamon**

1. Preheat oven to 350°. Cut buns into 1-in. cubes; place half in a 13x9-in. baking dish coated with cooking spray. Layer with cream cheese, bananas and remaining cubed buns.

2. In a large bowl, whisk eggs, milk, sugar, syrup and cinnamon; pour over top. Refrigerate, covered, 8 hours or overnight.

3. Remove from the refrigerator 30 minutes before baking. Bake, covered, 30 minutes. Bake, uncovered, 25-30 minutes longer or until a knife inserted near center comes out clean. Let stand 10 minutes before serving.

Spinach Bacon Brunch Pizza

Want to dazzle weekend guests? Serve this deep-dish breakfast pizza. The bacon, eggs, cheese and spinach will help everyone start the day off right.

—SHARON SKILDUM MAPLE GROVE, MN

PREP: 20 MIN. • **BAKE:** 45 MIN.
MAKES: 2 SERVINGS

- 1⅓ **cups biscuit/baking mix**
- ⅓ **cup water**
- 6 **eggs, lightly beaten**
- ⅔ **cup sour cream**
- ¾ **teaspoon garlic powder**
- ½ **teaspoon pepper**
- 2 **cups fresh baby spinach, chopped**
- 1 **cup (4 ounces) shredded cheddar cheese**
- 2 **green onions, chopped**
- 8 **bacon strips, cooked, crumbled and divided**

1. In a small bowl, combine biscuit mix and water to form a soft dough. Press onto the bottom and up the sides of a 8-in. deep-dish pie plate coated with cooking spray.

2. Bake at 400° for 6 minutes or until golden brown. Remove from the oven. Reduce heat to 375°.

3. In a small bowl, combine the eggs, sour cream, garlic powder and pepper. Stir in spinach, cheddar, green onions and half the bacon. Pour into crust. Sprinkle with remaining bacon. Bake for 40-45 minutes or until a knife inserted near center comes out clean.

Pesto Chicken Strata

Enjoy the hearty flavor of this strata when you want to serve something savory for brunch alongside the usual sweet rolls.

—**MICHAEL COHEN** LOS ANGELES, CA

PREP: 25 MIN. + CHILLING • **BAKE:** 40 MIN.
MAKES: 12 SERVINGS

- 1 **pound boneless skinless chicken thighs, cut into 1-inch pieces**
- ¾ **teaspoon salt, divided**
- ¾ **teaspoon coarsely ground pepper, divided**
- 1 **tablespoon plus ½ cup olive oil, divided**
- 1 **cup chopped fresh basil**
- 1½ **cups grated Parmesan cheese, divided**
- 1 **cup (4 ounces) shredded part-skim mozzarella cheese**
- ⅔ **cup pine nuts, toasted**
- 5 **garlic cloves, minced**
- 10 **eggs**
- 3 **cups 2% milk**
- 8 **cups cubed Italian bread**
  Additional chopped fresh basil leaves

1. Sprinkle chicken with ¼ teaspoon salt and ¼ teaspoon pepper. In a large skillet, heat 1 tablespoon oil over medium heat. Add chicken; cook and stir 6-8 minutes or until no longer pink. Drain.
2. In a large bowl, mix basil, 1 cup Parmesan cheese, mozzarella cheese, pine nuts and garlic. In another bowl, whisk eggs, milk and remaining oil, salt and pepper.
3. In a greased 13x9-in. baking dish, layer half of the bread cubes, a third of the cheese mixture and half of the chicken. Repeat layers. Top with remaining cheese mixture. Pour egg mixture over top; sprinkle with remaining Parmesan cheese. Refrigerate, covered, several hours or overnight.
4. Preheat oven to 350°. Remove strata from refrigerator while oven heats. Bake, uncovered, 40-50 minutes or until golden brown and a knife inserted near the center comes out clean. Let stand 5-10 minutes before serving. Sprinkle with additional basil.

NOTE *To toast nuts, bake in a shallow pan in a 350° oven for 5-10 minutes or cook in a skillet over low heat until lightly browned, stirring occasionally*

Pineapple & Cream Cheese Bread Pudding

Every time I take this creamy bread pudding to church or school, people ask for the recipe. You can change up the fruit or add maple syrup to make it your own.

—**LAURA ELLIS** SAUCIER, MS

PREP: 20 MIN. + CHILLING • **BAKE:** 25 MIN.
MAKES: 12 SERVINGS

- 1 **can (20 ounces) unsweetened pineapple chunks, undrained**
- 10 **cups cubed dinner rolls (about 17 rolls)**
- 1 **package (8 ounces) cream cheese, softened**
- 3 **tablespoons confectioners' sugar**
- 5 **eggs**
- 1 **can (14 ounces) sweetened condensed milk**
- ½ **cup heavy whipping cream**
- 2 **teaspoons vanilla extract**

SAUCE
- 1 **can (14 ounces) sweetened condensed milk**
- ¼ **cup butter, cubed**
- 1½ **teaspoons vanilla extract**

1. Drain pineapple, reserving ⅓ cup juice. Place half of the bread cubes in a greased 13x9-in. baking dish. In a small bowl, beat cream cheese and confectioners' sugar until smooth; drop by tablespoonfuls over bread cubes. Top with remaining bread cubes and pineapple.
2. In a large bowl, whisk eggs, milk, cream, vanilla and reserved pineapple juice until blended; pour over pineapple. Refrigerate, covered, several hours or overnight.
3. Preheat oven to 350°. Remove bread pudding from refrigerator while oven heats. Bake, uncovered, 25-35 minutes or until lightly browned.
4. In a small saucepan, heat milk and butter until butter is melted. Remove from heat; stir in vanilla. Just before serving, drizzle over warm bread pudding.

PESTO CHICKEN STRATA

APPLE, CHEDDAR &
BACON BREAD PUDDING

FREEZE IT

Apple, Cheddar & Bacon Bread Pudding

I first had this dish at a bridal brunch many years ago. It was so delicious that I created my own version, and this is the result. Now I make it all the time!
—**MELISSA MILLWOOD** LYMAN, SC

PREP: 30 MIN. + CHILLING • **BAKE:** 45 MIN.
MAKES: 9 SERVINGS

- 3 **tablespoons butter**
- 2 **medium apples, peeled and chopped**
- ¼ **cup packed brown sugar**
- 6 **cups cubed day-old French bread**
- 1 **pound bacon strips, cooked and crumbled**
- 1½ **cups (6 ounces) shredded sharp cheddar cheese**
- 5 **eggs**
- 2¼ **cups 2% milk**
- ½ **teaspoon ground cinnamon**
- ¼ **teaspoon salt**
SAUCE
- 1 **cup maple syrup**
- ½ **cup chopped walnuts**

1. In a large skillet, heat butter over medium heat. Add apples; cook and stir 2-3 minutes or until crisp-tender. Reduce heat to medium-low; stir in brown sugar. Cook, uncovered, 8-10 minutes or until apples are tender, stirring occasionally. Cool completely.

2. In a greased 8-in.-square baking dish, layer half of each of the following: bread, bacon, apples and cheese. Repeat layers. In a large bowl, whisk eggs, milk, cinnamon and salt; pour over top. Refrigerate, covered, several hours or overnight.

3. Preheat oven to 350°. Remove bread pudding from refrigerator; uncover and let stand while oven heats. Bake 45-55 minutes or until puffed, golden and a knife inserted near the center comes out clean. Let stand 15 minutes before serving.

4. In a microwave-safe bowl, microwave syrup and walnuts until warmed, stirring once. Serve bread pudding with sauce.

FREEZE OPTION *After assembling, cover and freeze bread pudding. To use, partially thaw in refrigerator overnight. Remove from refrigerator 30 minutes before baking. Preheat oven to 350°. Bake and serve bread pudding with sauce as directed.*

Smoked Salmon-Potato Brunch Bake

The two different types of potatoes, fresh herbs and different textures make this brunch bake both unique and special.
—**VICTORIA JOHNSON** GILBERT, AZ

PREP: 35 MIN. + CHILLING • **BAKE:** 1 HOUR
MAKES: 9 SERVINGS

- 2 **tablespoons olive oil**
- 1 **medium russet potato, peeled and cut into ½-inch cubes**
- 1 **medium sweet potato, peeled and cut into ½-inch cubes**
- 1 **medium sweet red pepper, finely chopped**
- ½ **cup finely chopped red onion**
- 6 **eggs**
- 1½ **cups half-and-half cream**
- 1 **green onion, finely chopped**
- 2 **teaspoons snipped fresh dill or ¾ teaspoon dill weed**
- 2 **teaspoons Dijon mustard**
- ½ **teaspoon lemon-herb seasoning**
- ¼ **teaspoon coarsely ground pepper**
- 2 **cups day-old cubed bread**
- 8 **ounces smoked salmon fillets, cut into 1-inch pieces**
- 4 **ounces cream cheese, cut into ½-inch cubes**
  Minced fresh chives and dill

1. In a large skillet, heat oil over medium heat. Add russet potato; cook 3 minutes. Add sweet potato, red pepper and onion; cook 4-6 minutes longer or until lightly browned. Reduce heat to medium-low; cook, covered, 4-6 minutes or until vegetables are tender. Cool to room temperature.

2. In a large bowl, whisk eggs, cream, green onion, dill, mustard, lemon-herb seasoning and pepper until blended. In a greased 8-in.-square baking dish, layer potato mixture, bread and salmon; dot with cream cheese. Pour egg mixture over top. Refrigerate, covered, several hours or overnight.

3. Preheat oven to 350°. Remove casserole from refrigerator while oven heats. Bake, uncovered, 60-70 minutes or until a knife inserted near the center comes out clean. Let stand 5-10 minutes before serving. Sprinkle with chives and dill.

Asparagus Phyllo Bake

I'm Greek and grew up wrapping everything in phyllo. When asparagus is in season, I bring out the phyllo dough and start baking.
—**BONNIE GEAVARAS-BOOTZ**
SCOTTSDALE, AZ

PREP: 25 MIN. • **BAKE:** 50 MIN.
MAKES: 12 SERVINGS

- 2 **pounds fresh asparagus, trimmed and cut into 1-inch pieces**
- 5 **eggs, lightly beaten**
- 1 **carton (15 ounces) ricotta cheese**
- 1 **cup (4 ounces) shredded Swiss cheese**
- 2 **tablespoons grated Parmesan cheese**
- 2 **garlic cloves, minced**
- ½ **teaspoon salt**
- ½ **teaspoon grated lemon peel**
- ½ **teaspoon pepper**
- ½ **cup slivered almonds, toasted**
- ¾ **cup butter, melted**
- 16 **sheets phyllo dough (14x9 inches)**

1. In a large saucepan, bring 8 cups water to a boil. Add asparagus; cook, uncovered, 30 seconds or just until asparagus turns bright green. Remove asparagus and immediately drop into ice water. Drain and pat dry. In a large bowl, mix the eggs, cheeses and seasonings; stir in almonds and asparagus.
2. Preheat oven to 375°. Brush a 13x9-in. baking dish with some of the butter. Unroll phyllo dough. Layer eight sheets of phyllo in prepared dish, brushing each with butter. Keep remaining phyllo covered with plastic wrap and a damp towel to prevent it from drying out.
3. Spread ricotta mixture over phyllo layers. Top with remaining phyllo sheets, brushing each with butter. Cut into 12 rectangles. Bake 50-55 minutes or until golden brown.

NOTE *To toast nuts, bake in a shallow pan in a 350° oven for 5-10 minutes or cook in a skillet over low heat until lightly browned, stirring occasionally.*

⑤INGREDIENTS

Corny Beef Brunch

My mother passed along her passion for cooking to me, my daughters and my grandchildren. One of my daughters shared this incredibly easy recipe with me. She made it for her first overnight guests after she was married.
—**KATHLEEN LUTZ** STEWARD, IL

PREP: 10 MIN. • **BAKE:** 35 MIN.
MAKES: 8-10 SERVINGS

- 3 **cans (14 ounces each) corned beef hash**
- 12 **slices (1 ounce each) American cheese**
- 12 **eggs**
- ½ **teaspoon pepper**

Spread hash in the bottom of a greased 13x9-in. baking dish. Layer cheese slices over hash. Beat eggs and pepper; pour over top. Bake at 350° for 35-40 minutes or until a knife inserted near the center comes out clean.

Croissant Breakfast Casserole

Turning croissants and marmalade into a classic overnight casserole makes a wonderful treat for family and guests the next morning.

—JOAN HALLFORD

NORTH RICHLAND HILLS, TX

PREP: 15 MIN. + CHILLING • **BAKE:** 25 MIN.
MAKES: 12 SERVINGS

- 1 jar (18 ounces) orange marmalade
- ½ cup apricot preserves
- ⅓ cup orange juice
- 3 teaspoons grated orange peel
- 6 croissants, split
- 5 eggs
- 1 cup half-and-half cream
- 1 teaspoon almond or vanilla extract
  Quartered fresh strawberries

1. In a small bowl, mix marmalade, preserves, orange juice and peel. Arrange croissant bottoms in a greased 13x9-in. baking dish. Spread with 1½ cups marmalade mixture. Add croissant tops.

2. In another bowl, whisk eggs, cream and extract; pour over croissants. Spoon remaining marmalade mixture over tops. Refrigerate, covered, overnight.

3. Preheat oven to 350°. Remove casserole from refrigerator while oven heats. Bake, uncovered, 25-30 minutes or until a knife inserted near the center comes out clean. Let stand 5 minutes before serving. Serve with strawberries.

Greek Breakfast Casserole

I frequently make this for Sunday brunch and save the leftovers for quick breakfasts later in the week. Add your own favorite veggies or cheese—the variations are endless.
—LAURI KNOX PINE, CO

PREP: 35 MIN. • **BAKE:** 45 MIN. + STANDING
MAKES: 6 SERVINGS

- ½ pound Italian turkey sausage links, casings removed
- ½ cup chopped green pepper
- 1 shallot, chopped
- 1 cup water-packed artichoke hearts, rinsed, drained and chopped
- 1 cup chopped fresh broccoli
- ⅓ cup sun-dried tomatoes (not packed in oil), chopped
- 6 eggs
- 6 egg whites
- 3 tablespoons fat-free milk
- ½ teaspoon Italian seasoning
- ¼ teaspoon garlic powder
- ¼ teaspoon pepper
- ⅓ cup crumbled feta cheese

1. Preheat oven to 350°. In a large skillet, cook sausage, green pepper and shallot over medium heat 8-10 minutes or until sausage is no longer pink, breaking up sausage into crumbles; drain. Transfer mixture to an 8-in.-square baking dish coated with cooking spray. Top with artichokes, broccoli and sun-dried tomatoes.

2. In a large bowl, whisk eggs, egg whites, milk and seasonings until blended; pour over top. Sprinkle with feta.

3. Bake, uncovered, 45-50 minutes or until a knife inserted near the center comes out clean. Let stand 10 minutes before serving.

FREEZE OPTION *Cool baked casserole; cover and freeze. To use, partially thaw in refrigerator overnight. Remove from refrigerator 30 minutes before baking. Preheat oven to 325°. Bake casserole, as directed until heated through and a thermometer inserted in center reads 165°.*

Fiesta Corn Bread & Sausage Strata

I like to break away from traditional breakfast bakes, so I experimented and came up with this sweet-savory corn bread and sausage egg bake. It's a breeze to prepare and a great make-ahead morning meal.
—ELLEN WOODHAM-JOHNSON MATTESON, IL

PREP: 20 MIN. + CHILLING • **BAKE:** 50 MIN.
MAKES: 8 SERVINGS

- 1 pound bulk pork sausage
- 1 medium onion, chopped
- 4 cups cubed corn bread
- ½ cup frozen corn
- 1 cup (4 ounces) shredded cheddar cheese
- 4 eggs
- 1¼ cups 2% milk
- ½ cup salsa
- ½ cup sour cream

1. In a large skillet, cook sausage and onion over medium heat 6-8 minutes or until no longer pink, breaking into crumbles; drain.

2. In a greased 13x9-in. baking dish, layer half of each of the following: corn bread, sausage mixture, corn and cheese. Repeat layers. In a small bowl, whisk eggs, milk, salsa and sour cream. Pour over layers. Refrigerate, covered, several hours or overnight.

3. Preheat oven to 325°. Remove strata from refrigerator while oven heats. Bake, uncovered, 50-60 minutes or until golden brown and a knife inserted near the center comes out clean. Let stand 5-10 minutes before serving.

TOP TIP

I save money by shredding cheese blocks myself and storing the shredded cheese in the freezer, so I have it at my fingertips whenever I need it.
—EVELYN O. PARMA, OH

FIESTA CORN BREAD & SAUSAGE STRATA

Broccoli-Mushroom Bubble Bake

I got bored with the same old breakfast casseroles served at our monthly moms' meeting, so I decided to create something new. Judging by the reactions of the other moms, this one's a keeper.

—**SHANNON KOENE** BLACKSBURG, VA

PREP: 20 MIN. • **BAKE:** 25 MIN.
MAKES: 12 SERVINGS

- 1 teaspoon canola oil
- ½ pound sliced fresh mushrooms, finely chopped
- 1 medium onion, finely chopped
- 1 tube (16.3 ounces) large refrigerated flaky biscuits
- 1 package (10 ounces) frozen broccoli with cheese sauce
- 3 eggs
- 1 can (5 ounces) evaporated milk
- 1 teaspoon Italian seasoning
- ½ teaspoon garlic powder
- ½ teaspoon salt
- ¼ teaspoon pepper
- 1½ cups (6 ounces) shredded Colby-Monterey Jack cheese

1. Preheat oven to 350°. In a large skillet, heat oil over medium-high heat. Add mushrooms and onion; cook and stir 4-6 minutes or until tender.
2. Cut each biscuit into eight pieces; place in a greased 13x9-in. baking dish. Top with mushroom mixture.
3. Cook broccoli with cheese sauce according to package directions. Spoon over mushroom mixture.
4. In a large bowl, whisk eggs, milk and seasonings; pour over top. Sprinkle with cheese. Bake 25-30 minutes or until golden brown.

GREEN CHILI EGG PUFF

Green Chili Egg Puff

Green chilies add a touch of Southwest flavor to this fluffy egg dish. The cottage cheese offers nice texture, and people always adore the gooey Monterey Jack cheese melted throughout.

—**LAUREL LESLIE** SONORA, CA

PREP: 15 MIN. • **BAKE:** 35 MIN.
MAKES: 12 SERVINGS

- 10 eggs
- ½ cup all-purpose flour
- 1 teaspoon baking powder
- ½ teaspoon salt
- 4 cups (16 ounces) shredded Monterey Jack cheese
- 2 cups (16 ounces) 4% cottage cheese
- 1 can (4 ounces) chopped green chilies

1. In a large bowl, beat eggs on medium-high speed for 3 minutes or until light and lemon-colored.

Combine the flour, baking powder and salt; gradually add to eggs and mix well. Stir in the cheeses and chilies.
2. Pour into a greased 13x9-in. baking dish. Bake, uncovered, at 350° for 35-40 minutes or until a knife inserted near the center comes out clean. Let stand for 5 minutes before serving.

HOW TO

GET LEMON-COLORED EGGS
❶ Beat eggs with an electric mixer on high speed for about 5 minutes.
❷ The eggs are ready when the volume of beaten eggs increases, the texture changes from liquid to thick and foamy and the color becomes a light yellow.

Prosciutto-Pesto Breakfast Strata

I'd never tried prosciutto before this recipe, and it instantly made me a big-time fan! The layers of flavor in this dish are brilliant, making it well worth the time and a must for your recipe box.

—VICKI ANDERSON FARMINGTON, MN

PREP: 25 MIN. + CHILLING • **COOK:** 50 MIN.
MAKES: 10 SERVINGS

- 2 cups 2% milk
- 1 cup white wine or chicken broth
- 35 slices French bread (½ inch thick)
- ¼ cup minced fresh basil
- ¼ cup minced fresh parsley
- 3 tablespoons olive oil
- ½ pound thinly sliced smoked Gouda cheese
- ½ pound thinly sliced prosciutto
- 3 medium tomatoes, thinly sliced
- ½ cup prepared pesto
- 4 eggs
- ½ cup heavy whipping cream
- ½ teaspoon salt
- ¼ teaspoon pepper

1. In a shallow bowl, combine the milk and wine. Dip both sides of bread in milk mixture; squeeze gently to remove excess liquid. Layer the bread slices in a greased 13x9-in. baking dish.

2. Sprinkle with basil and parsley; drizzle with oil. Layer with half of the cheese, half of the prosciutto and all of the tomatoes; drizzle with half of the pesto. Top with remaining cheese, prosciutto and pesto.

3. In a small bowl, whisk eggs, cream, salt and pepper until blended; pour over top. Refrigerate, covered, several hours or overnight.

4. Preheat oven to 350°. Remove strata from refrigerator while oven heats. Bake, uncovered, 50-60 minutes or until golden brown and a knife inserted near the center comes out clean. Let stand 5-10 minutes before serving.

Orange Breakfast Souffle with Dried Cherries

Our family often took this decadent souffle to a local park to celebrate Father's Day. It's easy to make the night before, pop in the oven the next morning and take it to go!

—SHARON RICCI MENDON, NY

PREP: 20 MIN. + CHILLING
BAKE: 45 MIN. + STANDING
MAKES: 9 SERVINGS

- ½ cup orange juice
- ¾ cup dried cherries, divided
- 6 eggs
- 2 cups 2% milk
- ¼ cup sugar
- 1 tablespoon grated orange peel
- 2 teaspoons vanilla extract
- 1 teaspoon ground cinnamon
- ¼ teaspoon salt
- 8 cups cubed brioche or egg bread
- 1½ cups (6 ounces) cubed Havarti cheese
- 1 cup maple syrup
  Confectioners' sugar

1. Pour orange juice over ½ cup cherries in a small bowl; let stand 15 minutes. In a large bowl, whisk eggs, milk, sugar, orange peel, vanilla, cinnamon and salt until blended. Stir in cherry mixture. Gently stir in bread cubes; transfer to a greased 8-in.-square baking dish. Sprinkle with cheese. Refrigerate, covered, several hours or overnight.

2. Preheat oven to 350°. Remove souffle from refrigerator while oven heats. Bake 45-55 minutes or until puffed, golden and a knife inserted near the center comes out clean. Let stand 10 minutes before cutting.

3. In a small saucepan, combine maple syrup and remaining cherries; heat through. Serve with souffle; dust with confectioners' sugar.

(5) INGREDIENTS

Breakfast Bread Pudding

I make sure to assemble this the day before our grandchildren come to visit so I can spend more time having fun with them instead of cooking!

—ALMA ANDREWS LIVE OAK, FL

PREP: 10 MIN. + CHILLING • **BAKE:** 40 MIN.
MAKES: 6-8 SERVINGS

- 12 slices white bread
- 1 package (8 ounces) cream cheese, cubed
- 12 eggs
- 2 cups milk
- ⅓ cup maple syrup
- ¼ teaspoon salt

1. Remove and discard crusts from bread; cut bread into cubes. Toss lightly with cream cheese cubes; place in a greased 13x9-in. baking pan. In a large bowl, beat eggs. Add milk, syrup and salt; mix well. Pour over bread mixture. Cover and refrigerate 8 hours or overnight.

2. Remove from the refrigerator 30 minutes before baking. Bake, uncovered, at 375° for 40-45 minutes or until a knife inserted near the center comes out clean. Let stand 5 minutes before cutting.

PROSCIUTTO-PESTO BREAKFAST STRATA

CHEESE & CRAB
BRUNCH BAKE

Cheese & Crab Brunch Bake

Who doesn't love a simply cheesy seafood casserole that can be pulled together in 30 minutes, refrigerated overnight and baked up the next morning?

—JOYCE CONWAY WESTERVILLE, OH

PREP: 30 MIN. + CHILLING • **BAKE:** 50 MIN.
MAKES: 12 SERVINGS

- 2 tablespoons Dijon mustard
- 6 English muffins, split
- 8 ounces lump crabmeat, drained
- 2 tablespoons lemon juice
- 2 teaspoons grated lemon peel
- 2 cups (8 ounces) shredded white cheddar cheese
- 12 eggs
- 1 cup half-and-half cream
- 1 cup 2% milk
- ½ cup mayonnaise
- 1 teaspoon salt
- ½ teaspoon cayenne pepper
- ½ teaspoon pepper
- 2 cups (8 ounces) shredded Swiss cheese
- 1 cup grated Parmesan cheese
- 4 green onions, chopped
- ¼ cup finely chopped sweet red pepper
- ¼ cup finely chopped sweet yellow pepper

1. Spread the mustard over bottom half of muffins. Place in a greased 13x9-in. baking dish. Top with crab, lemon juice and peel. Sprinkle with cheddar cheese. Top with muffin tops; set aside.
2. In a large bowl, whisk eggs, cream, milk, mayonnaise, salt, cayenne and pepper. Pour over muffins; sprinkle with Swiss cheese, Parmesan cheese, onions and peppers. Cover and refrigerate overnight.
3. Remove from the refrigerator 30 minutes before baking. Preheat oven to 375°. Cover and bake 30 minutes. Uncover; bake 20-25 minutes longer or until set. Let stand 5 minutes before serving.

Breakfast Kugel

Noodle dishes are always a family favorite in our house. This dish, packed with apples and raisins, tastes wonderful on a cool morning.

—CAROL MILLER NORTHUMBERLAND, NY

PREP: 20 MIN. • **BAKE:** 1 HOUR + STANDING
MAKES: 12 SERVINGS

- 3 cups (24 ounces) 4% cottage cheese
- 1 teaspoon vanilla extract
- ¼ teaspoon salt
- 5 medium tart apples, peeled and thinly sliced
- 1 teaspoon ground cinnamon
- 2 cups applesauce
- 2 cups raisins
- 1 package (16 ounces) lasagna noodles, cooked and drained
- 1 cup (4 ounces) shredded cheddar cheese

1. In a blender, combine the cottage cheese, vanilla and salt; cover and process until smooth. Toss apples with cinnamon.
2. Combine applesauce and raisins; spread ¾ cup into a greased 13x9-in. baking dish. Layer with a fourth of the noodles, and a third of the applesauce mixture, cottage cheese mixture and apples. Repeat layers twice. Top with remaining noodles; sprinkle with cheddar cheese.
3. Cover and bake at 350° for 60-70 minutes or until apples are tender. Let stand for 15 minutes before cutting.

⑤ INGREDIENTS **FAST FIX**
Picante Omelet Pie

My daughter loves this tasty egg bake. She visits every week before church, so I serve it often.

—PHYLLIS CARLSON GARDNER, KS

START TO FINISH: 30 MIN.
MAKES: 6 SERVINGS

- ½ cup picante sauce
- 1 cup (4 ounces) shredded Monterey Jack cheese
- 1 cup (4 ounces) shredded cheddar cheese
- 6 eggs
- 1 cup (8 ounces) sour cream
  Tomato slices and minced fresh cilantro, optional

1. Pour the picante sauce into a lightly greased 9-in. pie plate. Sprinkle with cheeses; set aside. In a blender, combine eggs and sour cream; cover and process until smooth. Pour over the cheese.
2. Bake at 375° for 20-25 minutes or until a knife inserted near the center comes out clean. Let stand 5 minutes before cutting. Garnish with tomato and cilantro if desired.

Baked French Toast with Strawberries

I love French toast, but it's hard to make when you're feeding a big group. This recipe is my answer to the dilemma, especially when you throw in any fruit that is currently in season. The sweet pecan topping is the best part!

—**DAVID STELZL** WAXHAW, NC

PREP: 20 MIN. + CHILLING
BAKE: 40 MIN. + STANDING
MAKES: 12 SERVINGS

- 12 **slices day-old French bread (1 inch thick)**
- 6 **eggs**
- 1½ **cups 2% milk**
- 1 **cup half-and-half cream**
- 2 **tablespoons maple syrup**
- 1 **teaspoon vanilla extract**
- ½ **teaspoon ground cinnamon**
- ¼ **teaspoon ground nutmeg**

TOPPING

- 1 **cup packed brown sugar**
- ½ **cup butter, melted**
- 2 **tablespoons maple syrup**
- 1 **cup chopped pecans**
- 4 **cups chopped fresh strawberries**
  Additional maple syrup

1. Place bread in a single layer in a greased 13x9-in. baking dish. In a large bowl, whisk eggs, milk, cream, syrup, vanilla, cinnamon and nutmeg; pour over bread. For topping, in a small bowl, mix brown sugar, butter and syrup; stir in pecans. Spread over bread. Refrigerate, covered, overnight.
2. Preheat oven to 350°. Remove French toast from refrigerator while oven heats. Bake, uncovered, 40-50 minutes or until a knife inserted near the center comes out clean. Let stand 10 minutes before serving. Serve with strawberries and additional syrup.

BAKED FRENCH TOAST WITH STRAWBERRIES

**VALERY ANDERSON'S CRANBERRY
CORN BREAD CASSEROLE** *PAGE 104*

Side Dishes

SO YOU'VE GOT THE REST OF THE MEAL PLANNED—NOW FOR SIDES!
TURN HERE TO PERFECTLY ROUND THINGS OUT.

HOPE HUGGINS' CRUMB-TOPPED BROCCOLI BAKE
PAGE 98

STEPHANIE SORBIE'S TWO-CHEESE MAC 'N' CHEESE
PAGE 104

ELISABETH LARSEN'S SUMMER VEGETABLE COBBLER *PAGE 102*

Scalloped Sweet Corn Casserole

This is my Grandma Ostendorf's corn recipe I grew up enjoying.
—**LONNIE HARTSTACK** CLARINDA, IA

PREP: 25 MIN. • **BAKE:** 50 MIN.
MAKES: 8 SERVINGS

- 4 teaspoons cornstarch
- ⅔ cup water
- ¼ cup butter, cubed
- 3 cups fresh or frozen corn
- 1 can (5 ounces) evaporated milk
- ¾ teaspoon plus 1½ teaspoons sugar, divided
- ½ teaspoon plus ¾ teaspoon salt, divided
- 3 eggs
- ¾ cup 2% milk
- ¼ teaspoon pepper
- 3 cups cubed bread
- 1 small onion, chopped
- 1 cup Rice Krispies, slightly crushed
- 3 tablespoons butter, melted

1. Preheat oven to 350°. In a small bowl, mix cornstarch and water until smooth. In a large saucepan, heat butter over medium heat. Stir in corn, evaporated milk, ¾ teaspoon sugar and ½ teaspoon salt; bring just to a boil. Stir in cornstarch mixture; return to a boil, stirring constantly. Cook and stir 1-2 minutes or until thickened; cool slightly.
2. In a large bowl, whisk eggs, milk, pepper and the remaining sugar and salt until blended. Stir in bread, onion and corn mixture. Transfer to a greased 8-in.-square or 1½-qt. baking dish.
3. Bake, uncovered, 40 minutes. In a bowl, toss Rice Krispies with melted butter; sprinkle on top. Bake 10-15 minutes longer or until golden brown.
FREEZE OPTION *Cool unbaked casserole, reserving Rice Krispies topping for baking; cover and freeze. To use, partially thaw in refrigerator overnight. Remove from refrigerator 30 minutes before baking. Preheat oven to 350°. Bake casserole as directed, increasing time as necessary to heat through and for a thermometer inserted in center to read 165°.*

CRUMB-TOPPED BROCCOLI BAKE

Crumb-Topped Broccoli Bake

Broccoli is one of the main crops grown in my area. This recipe has pleased just about everyone who has tried it, including some who said they didn't like broccoli.
—**HOPE HUGGINS** SANTA CRUZ, CA

PREP: 20 MIN. • **BAKE:** 50 MIN.
MAKES: 6 SERVINGS

- ¼ cup chopped onion
- 2 tablespoons butter
- 2 tablespoons all-purpose flour
- ½ cup milk
- 1 jar (8 ounces) process cheese sauce
- 2 packages (10 ounces each) frozen broccoli cuts
- 3 eggs, lightly beaten
- ½ cup crushed butter-flavored crackers (about 12 crackers), divided
  Salt and pepper to taste

1. In a large saucepan, saute onion in butter until tender. Stir in flour until blended. Gradually stir in milk. Bring to a boil; cook and stir for 2 minutes or until thickened. Reduce heat; stir in cheese sauce until smooth. Remove from heat.
2. Cook broccoli according to package directions; drain and place in a bowl. Add cheese sauce mixture, eggs, ¼ cup cracker crumbs, salt and pepper.
3. Transfer to a greased 1½-qt. baking dish; sprinkle with remaining cracker crumbs. Place dish in a larger baking pan. Fill pan with hot water to a depth of 1 in. Bake, uncovered, at 350° for 50 minutes or until a thermometer reads 160°.

DID YOU KNOW?

If you prefer to buy fresh broccoli and freeze it on your own, try blanching broccoli first to keep it from getting soggy when reheated (and to lock in vitamins).

Tex-Mex Summer Squash Casserole

Mild-flavored yellow squash gets a big boost from chilies, jalapenos and red onion in this side dish. You can substitute zucchini for the yellow squash, too.
—TOMMY LOMBARDO EUCLID, OH

PREP: 15 MIN. • **BAKE:** 40 MIN. + STANDING
MAKES: 10 SERVINGS

- 7 medium yellow summer squash, sliced (about 10 cups)
- 2¼ cups (9 ounces) shredded cheddar cheese, divided
- 1 medium onion, chopped
- 1 can (4 ounces) chopped green chilies
- 1 can (4 ounces) diced jalapeno peppers, drained
- ¼ cup all-purpose flour
- ½ teaspoon salt
- ¾ cup salsa
- 4 green onions, sliced
- ¼ cup chopped red onion

1. Preheat oven to 400°. In a large bowl, combine squash, ¾ cup cheese, onion, chilies and jalapenos. Sprinkle with flour and salt; toss to combine.

2. Transfer to a greased 13x9-in. baking dish. Bake, covered, 30-40 minutes or until squash is tender.
3. Spoon the salsa over top; sprinkle with remaining 1½ cups cheese. Bake, uncovered, 10-15 minutes longer or until golden brown. Let stand 10 minutes. Top with green and red onions before serving.

Coconut-Bourbon Sweet Potatoes

For those who firmly state they're not sweet potato fans because of the taste or texture, the rich addition of coconut, bourbon and spices ensures this dish will win them over.
—REBECCA ANDERSON DRIFTWOOD, TX

PREP: 25 MIN. • **BAKE:** 35 MIN.
MAKES: 14 SERVINGS

- 8 cups mashed sweet potatoes
- ¾ cup half-and-half cream
- ½ cup packed brown sugar
- ½ cup bourbon
- 2 eggs
- ¼ cup honey
- 3 teaspoons vanilla extract
- 1¼ teaspoons ground cinnamon
- ¼ teaspoon salt
- 1 tablespoon molasses, optional
- ½ teaspoon ground cardamom, optional
- 1 cup flaked coconut
- ¾ cup golden raisins
- 1½ cups miniature marshmallows

TOPPING
- ½ cup all-purpose flour
- ½ cup packed brown sugar
- 1 teaspoon ground cinnamon
- ⅓ cup butter, melted
- 1 cup chopped pecans

1. In a large bowl, combine the first nine ingredients; add molasses and cardamom if desired. Stir in coconut and raisins. Transfer to a greased 13x9-in. baking dish; sprinkle with marshmallows.
2. In a small bowl, combine the flour, brown sugar and cinnamon. Add butter; mix until crumbly. Stir in pecans; sprinkle over marshmallows.
3. Bake, uncovered, at 350° for 35-40 minutes or until heated through and topping is golden brown.

⑤ INGREDIENTS

Scalloped Oysters

This recipe is a tradition in my husband's family. It's so easy to prepare, and everyone always loves it.
—MARTY RUMMEL TROUT LAKE, WA

PREP: 10 MIN. • **BAKE:** 25 MIN.
MAKES: 12 SERVINGS

- 6 eggs, beaten
- 1 quart half-and-half cream
- ¼ teaspoon pepper
- 4 cans (8 ounces each) whole oysters, drained
- 2 cups crushed butter-flavored crackers (about 50 crackers)

In a large bowl, combine the eggs, cream and pepper. Stir in oysters and crackers. Pour into 12 greased 6-oz. ramekins or custard cups; place on a baking sheet. Bake at 350° for 25-30 minutes or until a knife inserted near the center comes out clean.
NOTE Scalloped Oysters may also be baked in a 13x9-in. baking dish for 55-65 minutes or until a knife inserted near the center comes out clean.

TEX-MEX SUMMER SQUASH CASSEROLE

FAVORITE CHEESY
POTATOES

Minted Parsnip Souffles

Elegant parsnip souffles make wonderful use of a root vegetable that is often overlooked. The subtle mint pairs well with a variety of meats.
—**CATHERINE WILKINSON** DEWEY, AZ

PREP: 50 MIN. • **BAKE:** 20 MIN.
MAKES: 6 SERVINGS

- 3 eggs
- 3 tablespoons butter, divided
- 3 tablespoons all-purpose flour, divided
- 1½ pounds medium parsnips, peeled and sliced
- 2 tablespoons finely chopped onion
- ½ cup water
- 2 teaspoons lemon juice
- 3 tablespoons sugar
- 1 teaspoon salt
- 1 cup half-and-half cream
- 2 tablespoons minced fresh mint

1. Separate eggs; let stand at room temperature for 30 minutes. Grease six 8-oz. ramekins with 1 tablespoon butter and dust with 1 tablespoon flour.
2. Place the parsnips, onion and water in a large microwave-safe bowl. Cover and microwave on high for 5-7 minutes or until parsnips are tender. Let stand for 5 minutes; drain. Place parsnip mixture and lemon juice in a food processor; cover and process until blended. Set aside.
3. In a small saucepan over medium heat, melt remaining butter. Stir in the sugar, remaining flour and salt until blended. Gradually whisk in cream. Bring to a boil, stirring constantly. Cook and stir 1-2 minutes longer or until thickened. Transfer to a large bowl; stir in mint.
4. Stir a small amount of hot mixture into egg yolks; return all to the bowl, stirring constantly. Allow to cool slightly. Stir in parsnip mixture.
5. In another bowl with clean beaters, beat egg whites until stiff peaks form. Stir a fourth of the egg whites into egg yolk mixture until no white streaks remain. Fold in the remaining egg whites until combined. Transfer to prepared dishes.
6. Bake at 350° for 20-25 minutes or until the tops are puffed and center appears set. Serve immediately.

FREEZE IT
Favorite Cheesy Potatoes

My kids, husband and nephews all love these potatoes. I make a large batch in disposable pans and serve them at get-togethers—the holidays aren't the same without them.
—**BRENDA SMITH** CURRAN, MI

PREP: 30 MIN. • **BAKE:** 45 MIN.
MAKES: 12 SERVINGS (⅔ CUP EACH)

- 3½ pounds potatoes (about 7 medium), peeled and cut into ¾-inch cubes
- 1 can (10½ ounces) condensed cream of potato soup, undiluted
- 1 cup French onion dip
- ¾ cup 2% milk
- ⅔ cup sour cream
- 1 teaspoon minced fresh parsley
- ¼ teaspoon salt
- ¼ teaspoon pepper
- 1 package (16 ounces) process cheese (Velveeta), cubed
  Additional minced fresh parsley

1. Preheat oven to 350°. Place the potatoes in a Dutch oven; add water to cover. Bring to a boil. Reduce heat; cook, uncovered, 8-12 minutes or until tender. Drain. Cool slightly.
2. In a large bowl, mix soup, onion dip, milk, sour cream, parsley, salt and pepper; gently fold in potatoes and cheese. Transfer to a greased 13x9-in. baking dish.
3. Bake, covered, 30 minutes. Uncover; bake 15-20 minutes longer or until heated through and cheese is melted. Just before serving, stir to combine and sprinkle with additional parsley. (Potatoes will thicken upon standing.)
FREEZE OPTION *Cover and freeze unbaked casserole. To use, partially thaw in refrigerator overnight. Remove from refrigerator 30 minutes before baking. Preheat oven to 350°. Cover casserole with foil; bake as directed, increasing covered time to 1¼ to 1½ hours or until heated through and a thermometer inserted in center reads 165°. Uncover; bake 15-20 minutes longer or until lightly browned. Just before serving, stir to combine and, if desired, sprinkle with additional parsley.*

Baked Two-Cheese & Bacon Grits

To a Southerner, grits are a true staple. When you combine them with bacon and cheese, even Northerners will be asking for a second helping.

—MELISSA ROGERS TUSCALOOSA, AL

PREP: 25 MIN. • BAKE: 40 MIN. + STANDING
MAKES: 12 SERVINGS

- 6 thick-sliced bacon strips, chopped
- 3 cups water
- 3 cups chicken stock
- 1 teaspoon garlic powder
- ½ teaspoon pepper
- 2 cups quick-cooking grits
- 12 ounces process cheese (Velveeta), cubed (about 2⅓ cups)
- ½ cup butter, cubed
- ½ cup 2% milk
- 4 eggs, lightly beaten
- 2 cups (8 ounces) shredded white cheddar cheese

1. Preheat oven to 350°. In a large saucepan, cook bacon over medium heat until crisp, stirring occasionally. Remove pan from heat. Remove bacon with a slotted spoon; drain on paper towels.
2. Add water, stock, garlic powder and pepper to bacon drippings; bring to a boil. Slowly stir in grits. Reduce heat to medium-low; cook, covered, 5-7 minutes or until thickened, stirring occasionally. Remove from heat.
3. Add process cheese and butter; stir until melted. Stir in milk. Slowly stir in eggs until blended. Transfer to a greased 13x9-in. baking dish. Sprinkle with bacon and shredded cheese. Bake, uncovered, 40-45 minutes or until edges are golden brown and cheese is melted. Let stand 10 minutes before serving.

FREEZE OPTION *Cool unbaked casserole; cover and freeze. To use, partially thaw in refrigerator overnight. Remove casserole from refrigerator 30 minutes before baking. Preheat oven to 350°. Bake grits as directed, increasing time to 50-60 minutes or until heated through and a thermometer inserted in center reads 165°.*

Broccoli and Carrot Cheese Bake

A cheesy sauce makes vegetables so much more appealing to my crowd. This side dish will please and win over even the pickiest veggie-phobics.

—TRISHA KRUSE EAGLE, ID

PREP: 25 MIN. • BAKE: 30 MIN. + STANDING
MAKES: 9 SERVINGS

- 2 cups thinly sliced fresh carrots
- 2 cups fresh broccoli florets
- 3 eggs
- 2 cups 2% milk
- ¼ cup butter, melted
- ½ teaspoon salt
- ¼ teaspoon ground nutmeg
- ¼ teaspoon pepper
- 1½ cups (6 ounces) grated Gruyere or Swiss cheese, divided
- 6 cups cubed egg bread

1. Place carrots and broccoli in a steamer basket; place in a large saucepan over 1 in. of water. Bring to a boil; cover and steam 3-4 minutes or until crisp-tender.
2. Preheat oven to 325°. In a large bowl, whisk eggs, milk, butter, salt, nutmeg and pepper. Stir in vegetables and 1 cup cheese. Gently stir in bread.
3. Transfer to a greased 11x7-in. baking dish; sprinkle with remaining cheese. Bake, uncovered, 30-35 minutes or until a knife inserted near the center comes out clean. Let stand 10 minutes before serving.

TO MAKE AHEAD *This recipe can be made a day ahead; cover and refrigerate. Remove from the refrigerator 30 minutes before baking. Bake as directed.*

TOP TIP

Instead of covering my casserole dishes with aluminum foil when I take them to potlucks, I put them in clear plastic oven bags and close with a twist tie. The bags trap any spills, won't melt and allow people to see what's inside.

—**CARLENE H.** CROSSVILLE, TN

BROCCOLI AND CARROT CHEESE BAKE

Summer Vegetable Cobbler

Here's a comforting veggie-filled side that uses a lot of garden produce. If you want to switch it up, substitute different squashes, like pattypan and crookneck, for the zucchini.

—ELISABETH LARSEN PLEASANT GROVE, UT

PREP: 40 MIN. • **BAKE:** 25 MIN.
MAKES: 4 SERVINGS

- 2 tablespoons butter
- 3 small zucchini, sliced
- 1 small sweet red pepper, finely chopped
- 1 small onion, finely chopped
- 2 garlic cloves, minced
- 2 tablespoons all-purpose flour
- 1 cup 2% milk
- ½ teaspoon salt
- ¼ teaspoon pepper

BISCUIT TOPPING
- 1 cup all-purpose flour
- 1 teaspoon baking powder
- ½ teaspoon salt
- 3 tablespoons cold butter
- ¼ cup shredded Parmesan cheese
- 3 tablespoons minced fresh basil
- ⅔ cup 2% milk

1. Preheat oven to 400°. In a large skillet, heat butter over medium-high heat. Add zucchini, red pepper and onion; cook and stir 10-12 minutes or until zucchini is crisp-tender. Add garlic; cook 1 minute longer.
2. In a small bowl, whisk flour, milk, salt and pepper; stir into vegetables. Bring to a boil, stirring constantly; cook and stir 2-3 minutes or until sauce is thickened. Spoon into a greased 8-in.-square baking dish.
3. For topping, in a small bowl, whisk flour, baking powder and salt. Cut in butter until mixture resembles coarse crumbs. Stir in cheese and basil. Add milk; stir just until moistened. Drop by rounded tablespoonfuls over filling. Bake 25-30 minutes or until filling is bubbly and biscuits are golden brown.

PARMESAN KALE CASSEROLE

Parmesan Kale Casserole

I tried coming up with a creative way to use kale, and the result was a cheesy casserole. When my husband sampled it, he absolutely loved it. Bits of summer sausage add heartiness.

—DIANA JOHNSON AUBURN, WA

PREP: 10 MIN. • **BAKE:** 25 MIN.
MAKES: 6 SERVINGS

- 1½ cups heavy whipping cream
- ½ cup finely chopped summer sausage
- 3 garlic cloves, minced
- 2 packages (16 ounces each) frozen cut kale, thawed and squeezed dry (about 3 cups total)
- ¾ cup panko (Japanese) bread crumbs
- ¾ cup grated Parmesan cheese

1. Preheat oven to 350°. In a large skillet, combine cream, sausage and garlic; bring to a boil. Reduce heat; simmer, uncovered, 3-5 minutes or until slightly thickened. Stir in the kale. Add bread crumbs and cheese; toss to combine.
2. Transfer to a greased 8-in.-square baking dish. Bake 25-30 minutes or until edges are golden brown.

Scalloped Pineapple Casserole

My family can't get enough of this sweet and satisfying bake. It seem to disappear quickly whenever I prepare it.

—JUDY HOWLE COLUMBUS, MS

PREP: 15 MIN. • **BAKE:** 40 MIN.
MAKES: 6 SERVINGS

- ¾ cup butter, softened
- 1¼ cups sugar
- 3 eggs
- 1 can (20 ounces) crushed pineapple, well drained
- 1½ teaspoons lemon juice
- 4 cups firmly packed cubed white bread (crusts removed)

1. Preheat oven to 350°. In a large bowl, cream butter and sugar until light and fluffy. Add eggs, one at a time, beating well after each addition. Stir in pineapple and lemon juice. Gently fold in bread cubes.
2. Spoon into a greased 2-qt. baking dish. Bake, uncovered, 40 to 45 minutes or until top is lightly golden. Serve warm.

Zucchini & Cheese Casserole

My daughter and I love zucchini, and this casserole uses plenty for a substantial side dish. For added appeal, I sometimes throw in fresh diced tomatoes.

—**RACHELLE STRATTON** ROCK SPRINGS, WY

PREP: 20 MIN.
BAKE: 25 MIN. + STANDING
MAKES: 6 SERVINGS

- 4 **tablespoons butter, divided**
- 6 **small zucchini, chopped (about 7 cups)**
- 1 **large onion, chopped**
- 1½ **cups crushed Rice Chex**
- 1 **cup (4 ounces) shredded Colby-Monterey Jack cheese**
- 2 **eggs, lightly beaten**
- 1 **teaspoon salt**
- ¼ **teaspoon pepper**

1. Preheat oven to 350°. In a large skillet, heat 2 tablespoons butter over medium-high heat. Add zucchini and onion; cook and stir 10-12 minutes or until crisp-tender. Transfer to a bowl; cool slightly.

2. In a microwave, melt remaining butter. Drizzle over the cereal and toss to coat.

3. Stir cheese, eggs, salt and pepper into zucchini mixture; transfer to a greased 8-in.-square baking dish. Sprinkle with cereal mixture.

4. Bake, uncovered, 25-30 minutes or until heated through. Let stand 10 minutes before serving.

Two-Cheese Mac 'n' Cheese

A lot of stories claim that mac 'n' cheese was created by Thomas Jefferson, Marco Polo or the cooks of China. My favorite theory? An Italian housewife invented it to introduce non-Italian Americans to macaroni.

—STEPHANIE SORBIE GLENDALE, AZ

PREP: 35 MIN. • **BAKE:** 35 MIN.
MAKES: 15 SERVINGS

- 1 package (16 ounces) spiral pasta
- 3 tablespoons butter
- 3 garlic cloves, minced, optional
- 3 tablespoons all-purpose flour
- ⅛ teaspoon pepper
  Dash salt
- 4 cups 2% milk
- 5 cups (20 ounces) shredded sharp cheddar cheese, divided
- 1 cup shredded Asiago cheese

1. In a Dutch oven, cook pasta according to package directions.
2. Meanwhile, in a large saucepan, melt butter over medium heat. Add garlic if desired; cook and stir for 1 minute. Stir in flour, pepper and salt until blended; cook and stir until golden brown, about 5 minutes. Gradually whisk in the milk, stirring until smooth. Bring to a boil; cook 2 minutes longer or until thickened.
3. Remove from heat. Stir in 4 cups cheddar cheese and Asiago cheese until melted. Mixture will thicken.
4. Preheat oven to 350°. Drain pasta; stir in cheese sauce. Transfer to a greased 13x9-in. baking dish. Sprinkle with remaining cheddar cheese.
5. Bake, uncovered, 35-40 minutes or until golden brown. Let stand 5 minutes before serving.

FREEZE IT
Cranberry Corn Bread Casserole

What could be better on a cold day than a warm casserole and creamy sweet corn bread put together? Since it starts with a mix, this side takes no time to make. Just bake, scoop and eat. Yum!

—VALERY ANDERSON STERLING HTS, MI

PREP: 15 MIN. • **BAKE:** 20 MIN.
MAKES: 9 SERVINGS

- ½ cup dried cranberries
- ½ cup boiling water
- 1 package (8½ ounces) corn bread/muffin mix
- 1 teaspoon onion powder
- ¼ teaspoon rubbed sage
- 1 egg
- 1 can (14¾ ounces) cream-style corn
- 2 tablespoons butter, melted
- ¼ cup chopped pecans
- ½ teaspoon grated orange peel

1. Place cranberries in a small bowl; cover with boiling water. Let stand for 5 minutes; drain and set aside.
2. In a small bowl, combine the muffin mix, onion powder and sage. In another bowl, whisk the egg, corn and butter; stir into dry ingredients just until moistened. Fold in the pecans, orange peel and cranberries.
3. Transfer to a greased 8-in.-square baking dish. Bake, uncovered, at 400° for 20-25 minutes or until set.
FREEZE OPTION *Cool baked corn bread in pan; cover and freeze. To use, partially thaw in refrigerator overnight. Remove from refrigerator 30 minutes before baking. Preheat oven to 350°. Reheat corn bread 10-12 minutes or until heated through.*

Brussels Sprouts au Gratin

In our house, Brussels sprouts have always been popular. When I topped them with a creamy sauce, Swiss cheese and bread crumbs, it became a new dinner tradition.
—GWEN GREGORY RIO OSO, CA

PREP: 30 MIN. • **BAKE:** 20 MIN.
MAKES: 6 SERVINGS

- 2 pounds fresh Brussels sprouts, quartered
- 1 tablespoon olive oil
- ½ teaspoon salt, divided
- ¼ teaspoon pepper, divided
- ¾ cup cubed sourdough or French bread
- 1 tablespoon butter
- 1 tablespoon minced fresh parsley
- 2 garlic cloves, coarsely chopped
- 1 cup heavy whipping cream
- ⅛ teaspoon crushed red pepper flakes
- ⅛ teaspoon ground nutmeg
- ½ cup shredded white sharp cheddar or Swiss cheese

1. Preheat oven to 450°. Place Brussels sprouts in a large bowl. Add oil, ¼ teaspoon salt and ⅛ teaspoon pepper; toss to coat. Transfer to two ungreased 15x10x1-in. baking pans. Roast 8-10 minutes or until lightly browned and crisp-tender. Reduce oven setting to 400°.

2. Meanwhile, place bread, butter, parsley and garlic in a food processor; pulse until fine crumbs form.

3. Place roasted sprouts in a greased 8-in.-square baking dish. In a small bowl, mix cream, pepper flakes, nutmeg, and remaining salt and pepper. Pour over Brussels sprouts; sprinkle with cheese. Top with crumb mixture. Bake, uncovered, 15-20 minutes or until bubbly and topping is lightly browned.

FREEZE IT

Harvest Squash Casserole

Flavored with autumn cranberries and pecans, this nutritious recipe works very well as a side dish next to roasted turkey or chicken.
—MARY ANN LEE CLIFTON PARK, NY

PREP: 35 MIN. • **BAKE:** 40 MIN.
MAKES: 10 SERVINGS

- 1 large butternut squash (about 6 pounds), peeled, seeded and cubed
- 1 large onion, finely chopped
- 1 tablespoon butter
- 2 garlic cloves, minced
- 3 eggs, lightly beaten
- 2 tablespoons sugar
- 2 teaspoons salt
- ½ teaspoon pepper
- 1 cup chopped fresh or frozen cranberries
- ¾ cup chopped pecans

TOPPING

- 2 cups soft whole wheat bread crumbs
- 2 tablespoons butter, melted

1. Place squash in a Dutch oven; cover with water. Bring to a boil. Reduce heat; cover and cook 15-20 minutes or just until tender. Drain. In a large bowl, mash squash and set aside.

2. Preheat oven to 350°. In a large nonstick skillet, saute onion in butter until tender. Add garlic; cook 1 minute longer. Add to squash. Stir in eggs, sugar, salt and pepper. Gently fold in cranberries and pecans. Transfer to a 13x9-in. baking dish coated with cooking spray.

3. For topping, combine bread crumbs and melted butter; sprinkle over top. Bake 40-45 minutes or until a knife inserted near the center comes out clean.

FREEZE OPTION *Cool unbaked casserole. Sprinkle with topping; cover and freeze. To use, partially thaw in refrigerator overnight. Remove from refrigerator 30 minutes before baking. Preheat oven to 350°. Bake casserole as directed, increasing time as necessary for a knife inserted near the center to come out clean.*

HOW TO

CHOP AN ONION

1 To quickly chop an onion, peel and cut in half from the root to the top. Leaving root attached, place flat side down on work surface.

2 Cut vertically through the onion, leaving the root end uncut.

3 Cut across the onion, discarding root end. The closer the cuts, the finer the onion will be chopped.

BRUSSELS SPROUTS AU GRATIN

BASIL CORN &
TOMATO BAKE

⅛ teaspoon salt
3 cups thinly sliced peeled tart
apples
4 tablespoons butter, divided

1. Place the sweet potatoes in a large saucepan and cover with water. Bring to a boil. Reduce heat; cover and simmer 30 minutes or until tender. Drain. When cool enough to handle, peel potatoes and cut into ½-in. slices.
2. Preheat oven to 375°. In a small bowl, combine brown sugar, walnuts, cinnamon and salt; set aside. In a large skillet, saute apples in 2 tablespoons butter 3-4 minutes or until tender.
3. In a greased 1½-qt. baking dish, layer half the sweet potatoes, apples and brown sugar mixture. Repeat layers.
4. Dot with remaining butter. Cover and bake 30 minutes. Uncover; bake 15 minutes longer or until bubbly.

Basil Corn &
Tomato Bake

When sweet Jersey corn is in season, I turn to this recipe. Studded with summer tomatoes, zucchini and fresh basil, it's a great choice for dinner, lunch or even brunch.
—**ERIN CHILCOAT** CENTRAL ISLIP, NY

PREP: 30 MIN. • **BAKE:** 45 MIN. + STANDING
MAKES: 10 SERVINGS

- 2 teaspoons olive oil
- 1 medium onion, chopped
- 2 eggs
- 1 can (10¾ ounces) reduced-fat reduced-sodium condensed cream of celery soup, undiluted
- 4 cups fresh or frozen corn
- 1 small zucchini, chopped
- 1 medium tomato, seeded and chopped
- ¾ cup soft whole wheat bread crumbs
- ⅓ cup minced fresh basil
- ½ teaspoon salt
- ½ cup shredded part-skim mozzarella cheese
  Additional minced fresh basil, optional

1. Preheat oven to 350°. In a small skillet, heat oil over medium heat. Add the onion; cook and stir until tender.

In a large bowl, whisk eggs and condensed soup until blended. Stir in vegetables, bread crumbs, basil, salt and onion. Transfer mixture to an 11x7-in. baking dish coated with cooking spray.
2. Bake, uncovered, 40-45 minutes or until bubbly. Sprinkle with cheese. Bake 5-10 minutes longer or until cheese is melted. Let stand 10 minutes before serving. If desired, sprinkle with additional basil.
NOTE *To make soft bread crumbs, tear bread into pieces and place in a food processor or blender. Cover and pulse until crumbs form. One slice of bread yields ½ to ¾ cup crumbs.*

Apple Sweet
Potato Bake

I've been cooking since I was 7 years old, and I still get excited when I find a recipe that is not only good, but quick and easy to make. This sweet and nutty side dish is the perfect example.
—**VALERIE WALKER** CANTON, IL

PREP: 45 MIN. • **BAKE:** 45 MIN.
MAKES: 6-8 SERVINGS

- 2½ pounds sweet potatoes
- ½ cup packed brown sugar
- ⅓ cup chopped walnuts
- 1 teaspoon ground cinnamon

Roasted
Cauliflower Mash

Here's a tempting alternative to traditional holiday sides of spuds or rice. Guests who don't detect the cauliflower might even think it's mashed potatoes!
—**JANE MCGLOTHREN** DAPHNE, AL

PREP: 30 MIN. • **BAKE:** 25 MIN.
MAKES: 10 SERVINGS

- 2 medium heads cauliflower, broken into florets
- ¼ cup olive oil
- 6 garlic cloves, minced
- 2 teaspoons Greek seasoning
- 1 cup (4 ounces) shredded sharp cheddar cheese
- ⅔ cup sour cream
- ½ cup crumbled cooked bacon
- ⅓ cup butter, cubed

1. In a large bowl, combine the cauliflower, oil, garlic and Greek seasoning. Transfer to a greased 15x10x1-in. baking pan. Bake, uncovered, at 425° for 15-20 minutes or until tender, stirring occasionally.
2. Transfer cauliflower to a large bowl. Mash cauliflower with cheese, sour cream, bacon and butter. Transfer to a greased 8-in.-square baking dish. Bake at 350° for 25-30 minutes or until heated through.

Twice-Baked Cheddar Potato Casserole

Bacon, cheddar and sour cream transform ordinary potatoes into this irresistible side dish. This is one of our family's favorites.

—**KYLE COX** SCOTTSDALE, AZ

PREP: 70 MIN. • **BAKE:** 15 MIN.
MAKES: 12 SERVINGS (⅔ CUP EACH)

- 8 medium baking potatoes (about 8 ounces each)
- ½ cup butter, cubed
- ⅔ cup sour cream
- ⅔ cup 2% milk
- 1 teaspoon salt
- ¾ teaspoon pepper
- 10 bacon strips, cooked and crumbled, divided
- 2 cups (8 ounces) shredded cheddar cheese, divided
- 4 green onions, chopped, divided

1. Preheat oven to 425°. Scrub potatoes; pierce several times with a fork. Bake 45-60 minutes or until tender. Remove from oven; reduce oven setting to 350°.

2. When potatoes are cool enough to handle, cut each potato lengthwise in half. Scoop out pulp and place in a large bowl; discard shells. Mash pulp with butter; stir in sour cream, milk, salt and pepper.

3. Reserve ¼ cup crumbled bacon for topping. Gently fold remaining bacon, 1 cup cheese and half of the green onions into potato mixture (do not overmix).

4. Transfer to a greased 11x7-in. baking dish. Top with the remaining cheese and green onions; sprinkle with reserved bacon. Bake 15-20 minutes or until heated through and cheese is melted.

TWICE-BAKED CHEDDAR POTATO CASSEROLE

General Index

This index lists every recipe by food category and/or major ingredient, so you can easily locate the recipes that best suit your tastes.

Alphabetical Index

This index lists every recipe in the book by title, making it easy to find your family's favorite dishes.